Audiovisual translation in the foreign language classroom: applications in the teaching of English and other foreign languages

Written by Jennifer Lertola

Published by Research-publishing.net, a not-for-profit association
Voillans, France, info@research-publishing.net

© 2019 by Jennifer Lertola

**Audiovisual translation in the foreign language classroom:
applications in the teaching of English and other foreign languages**

Written by Jennifer Lertola

Publication date: 2019/02/28

Typeset by Research-publishing.net
Cover design by © 2019 Raphaël Savina (raphael@savina.net)

ISBN13: 978-2-490057-25-2 (Ebook, PDF, colour)
ISBN13: 978-2-490057-26-9 (Ebook, EPUB, colour)
ISBN13: 978-2-490057-24-5 (Paperback - Print on demand, black and white)
Print on demand technology is a high-quality, innovative and ecological printing method; with which the book is never 'out of stock' or 'out of print'.

British Library Cataloguing-in-Publication Data.
A cataloguing record for this book is available from the British Library.

Legal deposit, UK: British Library.
Legal deposit, France: Bibliothèque Nationale de France - Dépôt légal: Février 2019.

Table of contents

Notes on contributors

Author

Jennifer Lertola, Ph.D., collaborates with the School of Languages and Literatures, Translation, and Interpreting of the University of Bologna and with the Department of Humanities of the University of Eastern Piedmont, Italy. Her main research interests include foreign language education, audiovisual translation, and distance learning. She is the author of various articles and chapters on audiovisual translation and language learning. She is a member of the Editorial Board of the journal "Translation and Translanguaging in Multilingual Contexts", published by John Benjamins, and co-editor along with Laura Incalcaterra McLoughlin and Noa Talaván for a special issue about audiovisual translation in applied linguistics.

Foreword

Maicol Formentelli, Ph.D. in Linguistics from the University of Pavia, is a lecturer of English Language and Linguistics at the University of Eastern Piedmont 'A. Avogadro'. His main research interests include the study of English varieties with a focus on sociolinguistic, pragmatic, and interactional aspects of language, the investigation of interpersonal relations in academic interactions in English as a lingua franca, and the analysis of film dialogue and audiovisual translation processes. Among his publications are the volumes "Taking Stance in English as a Lingua Franca" (Cambridge Scholars Publishing, 2017) and "The Languages of Dubbing. Mainstream Audiovisual Translation in Italy" (Peter Lang, 2014), edited with Maria Pavesi and Elisa Ghia.

Reviewers

Laura Incalcaterra McLoughlin, Ph.D., is Senior Lecturer in Italian Studies at the National University of Ireland, Galway. Her research interests are mainly in applied linguistics, audiovisual translation, language technologies, and e-learning. She is co-Director of the MA in Advanced Language Skills and Director of the Diploma in Italian Online. She participated in and led a number of nationally and internationally funded projects and has taken part in several international teaching assignments in Europe and beyond.

Noa Talaván is Associate Professor of English Studies and Translation at the Foreign Languages Department of the Universidad Nacional de Educación a Distancia (UNED), Spain. Her main field of research is audiovisual translation and foreign language education, in which she has been publishing an important number of articles and books since 2006.

Acknowledgements

This work started from the desire to investigate the applications of audiovisual translation in the foreign language classroom as a whole. The chance to carry out such investigations came with the development of an M.A. dissertation. Therefore, I would like to express my sincere gratitude to my supervisor, Dr Maicol Formentelli. Furthermore, I would like to thank Dr Laura Incalcaterra McLoughlin and Dr Noa Talaván for their valuable suggestions.

List of abbreviations and acronyms

- AD: Audio Description

- AV: Audiovisual

- AVT: Audiovisual Translation

- L1: First Language/Mother Tongue

- L2: Second Language

- LeViS: Learning via Subtitling (project)

- LvS: Learning via Subtitling (software)

- NUI: National University of Ireland

- UNED: Universidad Nacional de Educación a Distancia

- VISP: VIdeos for SPeaking

Foreword

The digital turn in the late 1990's and the rapid spread of fast Internet connections have left a permanent mark on contemporary society. One important effect of technological advancement is evident in the dramatic increase in the production and worldwide circulation of audiovisual materials, which has promoted the wide scale access and consumption of telecinematic products for entertainment, leisure, information gathering, and, more recently, language learning. Audiovisual translation too has benefitted from the introduction of digital technologies and, at the same time, has contributed substantially to this societal change by fostering the dissemination of foreign languages and cultures through subtitled and dubbed products.

Under the impulse of the Council of Europe and its educational policies aimed at promoting multilingualism among European citizens, some scholars inaugurated a new field of study to explore and uncover the potentials of audiovisual translation for language teaching and learning, a fruitful and promising area of research which has led to numerous studies developed by single European universities and to two important projects funded by the European Commission and involving a network of academic institutions: LeViS (2006-2008)[1] and ClipFlair (2011-2014)[2].

The main assumptions underlying research in this emerging field include the rich contextualised language input offered by original and translated audiovisual material and the motivating context fostered by multimodal texts, capable of entertaining and engaging learners in classroom activities, thus lowering their affective filter (Krashen, 1985) and facilitating second language acquisition. This

---

1. Learning via Subtitling: software and processes for developing language learning material based on film subtitling; http://levis.cti.gr

2. Foreign language learning through interactive revoicing and captioning of clips: www.clipflair.net

has led over the years to the implementation of learner-centred tasks based on interactive audiovisual translation activities to be carried out both individually and in groups, under the guidance of the teacher or independently to promote autonomous and cooperative language learning.

The main objective of the present volume is to systematically review the empirically-based experimental studies conducted in the last 20 years that have foregrounded the positive links between audiovisual translation tasks and foreign language learning, in order to offer a detailed and comprehensive picture of the state of the art. The book is organised in three main sections – *Captioning, Revoicing,* and *Combined captioning and revoicing* – followed by a concluding critical discussion of the main issues and some suggestions on promising strands for future research.

The first section is devoted to captioning, a general term used to indicate a wide range of writing activities on the screen, including "interlingual subtitles, […] captions for the deaf and hard-of-hearing, intertitles, annotations or speech bubbles" (Sokoli, 2018, p. 80). Experimental studies focussing on a variety of linguistic aspects have been carried out involving procedures of standard interlingual subtitling (from L2 to L1), the most developed line of research to date, but also reverse interlingual subtitles (from L1 to L2), and intralingual subtitles (from L2 to L2). Positive outcomes of learners' improvements are reported on incidental vocabulary acquisition, idiomatic expression retention, development of pragmatic awareness, listening comprehension skills, and writing and translation skills.

Then, the attention shifts to another major audiovisual translation mode, namely revoicing, and in particular to experimental research on reverse interlingual dubbing (oral translation of L1 spoken dialogue into L2), intralingual dubbing (voice repetition of original L1 spoken dialogue), the emerging narrative technique of audio description (a recount of what is shown on screen for the blind and visually impaired), and voice-over (asynchronous oral translation into L2 added a few seconds after the onset of L1 original dialogue). The findings show that revoicing tasks prove effective in improving learners' speaking skills, in particular pronunciation, intonation, awareness of prosodic features, and fluency. In addition, some of the studies on audio description tasks demonstrate that revoicing can stimulate metalinguistic reflection and contribute to the development of lexical and phraseological competence.

The following section presents a more recent strand of experimental research combining captioning and revoicing tasks, and pays attention to studies on combined reverse interlingual dubbing and subtitling (from L1 to L2) and, to a lesser extent, on combined intralingual captioning and revoicing (from L2 to L2). The number of studies discussed in this last part is necessarily more limited, but the findings confirm the positive results already reported in previous research, especially on learners' improvement of L2 written and oral production skills, general translation skills, and pragmatic awareness.

With its systematic, comprehensive and up-to-date review of more than 40 experimental studies, Lertola's volume constitutes a valuable reference book both for researchers who approach this area of study for the first time and for scholars who have already worked on audiovisual translation as an instrument for language learning. It illustrates a range of quantitative and qualitative methods and procedures used in data collection and analysis, including pre- and post-tests administered to experimental and control groups of learners, evaluation rubrics, participant observation, questionnaires and interviews, and discussion forums which capture not only the positive effects of audiovisual translation tasks on language learning, but also the opinions and impressions of teachers and students involved in the activities. The triangulation of data and methodologies testify to the rigorousness of the studies and the reliability of results, despite the often limited number of participants in the experiments.

The present book is also a useful point of reference for teachers who are willing to introduce innovative teaching practices in education, as it accurately describes a variety of tasks successfully implemented in different learning settings, including face-to-face, online, and blended contexts. It offers pedagogical models, guidelines, and suggestions, while at the same time it does not conceal the limitations and drawbacks inherent in audiovisual translation tasks that teachers should be aware of, such as the lack of ready-made activities (now partly overcome by the freely-accessible material designed in the ClipFlair project), the time-consuming selection of appropriate videos to meet students' interests and proficiency levels, the technological skills needed to use specific dubbing and subtitling software programmes, and the need for computers and an internet connection in the classroom.

All in all, Jennifer Lertola shows us how a pervasive component of our daily lives like telecinematic products can be successfully employed to develop audiovisual translation tasks to be integrated with traditional foreign language teaching activities. As the author reminds us in her final discussion, however, more research is needed, encompassing still under-investigated translation modes (for instance reverse interlingual subtitling and dubbing, intralingual subtitling, and combined intralingual captioning and revoicing) and, above all, a larger number of language combinations (so far English, Spanish, and Italian are the most represented languages with very few exceptions); but the path has been traced and the principal actors involved in this process of change have already welcomed the new educational perspectives.

Dr Maicol Formentelli
Università del Piemonte Orientale, Vercelli, Italy

Introduction

Rapid technological changes have given rise to new methods and opportunities in language learning. In the past two decades, interest has been growing in the integration of Audiovisual Translation (AVT) with a communicative approach to language learning and teaching. AVT indicates the transfer of verbal language in audiovisual media and it is usually used as an umbrella term which refers to *screen-translation, film translation, multimedia translation,* or *multimodal translation* (Bollettieri, Di Giovanni, & Rossato, 2014; Chiaro, 2009; Perego, 2005). AVT modes[1] can be divided into two main groups: captioning[2] (written language transfer procedures) and revoicing (oral language transfer procedures). These language transfer procedures can take place between two languages (interlingual) or within the same language (intralingual). Both captioning and revoicing tasks can be used effectively in second language acquisition[3].

Captioning allows learners to add the written translation (interlingual subtitling) or a condensed transcription (intralingual subtitling) of the original spoken language to an Audiovisual (AV) product. Captioning can foster listening,

---

1. The terms *mode* and *type* are used as synonyms in AVT research (Gambier, 2003). Other terms like *procedure, method,* and *technique* are employed as synonyms of *mode* and *type* (Pérez-González, 2014).

2. In AVT research and practice, the term *subtitling* is usually employed to indicate the AVT written type (Pérez González, 2009; Pérez-González, 2014). In this work, the term *captioning* is used – instead of *subtitling* – as hypernym to refer to "ANY thing done in terms of [...] writing on the screen" as proposed in the ClipFlair theoretical framework (Zabalbeascoa, Sokoli, & Torres, 2012, p. 18). As stated by Sokoli (2018), "[a]dding written words includes processes such as standard interlingual subtitling but it can also refer to inserting captions for the deaf and hard-of-hearing, intertitles, annotations or speech bubbles" (p. 79).

3. The term *second language acquisition* is employed as an umbrella term encompassing both second and foreign language acquisition. Unless otherwise specified, the terms *learning* and *acquisition* are used interchangeably. The term *second language* (L2) generally refers to another language, acquired in some measure after one's native language (L1), and this term can also indicate the study of a third or even fourth language. The defining condition is that an L1 has already been learned, in formal or informal educational settings. The term *foreign language* also indicates another language acquired to some measure, but it is differentiated from L2 since here learning usually takes place in a classroom context located outside the country or community where that language is spoken. Here within, the term *L2* will be used to indicate non-native language learning in the country where the L2 is spoken. In the past few years, however, the term *second language acquisition* has been more widely used to indicate the study of another language regardless of the environment in which it takes place, perhaps because "[t]he term 'second' is more neutral and it is totally free of the negative nuances that might be associated to 'foreign'" (Ma, 2009, p. 20).

reading, and writing as well as improve transferable skills. Revoicing offers learners the opportunity to enhance their speaking skills through dubbing, Audio Description (AD), and other voice-over tasks[4]. Dubbing allows learners to replace the voice of someone in an AV product with their own voice. Dubbing – also known in the professional practice as *lip-synchronised dubbing* – can prove to be more challenging for learners due to the synchronisation between spoken language and onscreen images. AD – which aims to assist visually impaired people – requires learners to provide a spoken account of relevant visual aspects of the AV product between stretches of the original spoken dialogue. Depending on the task undertaken, revoicing can also promote listening, reading, and writing skills. AVT activities are learner-centred tasks which can be carried out both individually or in groups, and thus have the potential to promote autonomous and cooperative learning.

Captioning and revoicing in language learning can be either standard or reverse (Table 1). Standard interlingual subtitling refers to spoken second language (L2) text translated into written first language (L1), while interlingual reverse subtitling refers to spoken L1 text translated into written L2. Intralingual subtitling is a condensed transcription in L2 of the original spoken language as in the professional practice[5]. With regard to revoicing, standard interlingual dubbing refers to spoken L2 text translated into spoken L1; while reverse dubbing refers to L1 spoken text translated into spoken L2. Although involving translation, standard interlingual dubbing is not frequently used in language learning. This may be because, contrary to standard interlingual subtitling, L2 input disappears completely from the final dubbed product. Finally, intralingual dubbing is a voice repetition of the original spoken language. While subtitling

---

4. The professional practice distinguishes a number of revoicing transfer methods: lip-synchronised dubbing, voice-over, narration, free commentary, and simultaneous interpreting (Pérez-González, 2014). This work follows the ClipFlair framework, which employs "the term *revoicing* to include all kinds of recording speech on video, including dubbing, voice over, audio description for the blind and visually impaired, free commentary, karaoke singing, or reciting" (Sokoli, 2018, p. 79).

5. In the professional practice, intralingual subtitling, also known as *captions* (Caimi, 2015) and referred to as bimodal, same language, or unilingual subtitling as well, "traditionally addressed at minority audiences, such as immigrants wishing to develop their proficiency in the language of the host community or viewers requiring written support to fully understand certain audiovisual texts [...] has now become almost synonymous with subtitling for the deaf and hard of hearing" (Pérez González, 2009, p. 15). However, subtitling for the deaf and hard-of-hearing also contains paralinguistic information otherwise not accessible to deaf people, while intralingual subtitling in language learning does not include paralinguistic information.

and dubbing remain the two most studied AVT techniques in language learning, audio description is gradually gaining scholars' attention[6].

Table 1.1. Main aspects of subtitling and dubbing in language learning

	AVT Modes	Standard	Reverse
Captioning	**Interlingual Subtitling** • Involves two languages: L2 and L1/(another L2). • Is the written translation of the original spoken language.	L2 => L1	L1=>L2
	Intralingual Subtitling • Involves one language: L2. • Is a condensed transcription of the original spoken language.	L2=>L2	-
Revoicing	**Interlingual Dubbing** • Involves two languages: L2 and L1/(another L2). • Is the oral translation of the original spoken language.	L2 => L1	L1=>L2
	Intralingual Dubbing • Involves one language: L2. • Is a voice repetition of the original spoken language.	L2=>L2	-

The AVT practice in language learning has raised interest among scholars and teachers. European institutions have also recognised the potential of AVT in language education by funding research-led projects like *Learning Via Subtitling* (LeViS)[7] (2006-2008) and ClipFlair[8] (2011-2014). LeViS developed a free subtitling software and activities specifically designed for language learning. These activities promote a 'hands-on' approach where multimedia represents

---

6. In addition, there has been an increasing interest in using AVT tasks in translator (and subtitler) training (Barbe, 1996; Incalcaterra McLoughlin, 2009b; Martí Ferriol & Martí Marco, 2016; Rundle, 2000; Williams & Thorne, 2000; to name a few). The analysis of this phenomenon goes beyond the scope of the present work.

7. http://levis.cti.gr/

8. http://clipflair.net/

the central aspect of an activity, rather than a marginal feature (Hadzilacos, Papadakis, & Sokoli, 2004). A final evaluation of the project through questionnaires has revealed that learners found the subtitling task motivating and suitable for the development of different skills; most of the respondents expressed that they would like to have these activities in their regular foreign language class (Sokoli, Zabalbeascoa, & Fountana, 2011). ClipFlair – based on the LeViS experience – aims at promoting language learning through interactive clip captioning and revoicing. Hence, learners have a wider range of activities at their disposal (Sokoli, 2015).

AVT modes differ greatly from one another and do not necessarily involve translation, as in the case of intralingual subtitling and dubbing (Orrego Carmona, 2013). In the broader terms of captioning and revoicing, ClipFlair includes any activity in which learners can interact with (and thus modify) a video by adding their writing or speech respectively. Three types of verbal learner responses can be identified in ClipFlair activities: repeating, rephrasing, or reacting.

> "*Repeating* refers to verbatim rendering of the verbal elements of the clip as literally as possible. *Rephrasing* means free rendering or rewording the text, and includes concepts such as "loose" paraphrase, gist, and summary. *Reacting* has to do with producing a new communicative contribution in response to a previous one" (Sokoli, 2018, p. 80, emphasis in the original).

ClipFlair activities can be employed successfully in face-to-face (Lertola & Mariotti, 2017), online (Incalcaterra McLoughlin & Lertola, 2015), or blended learning contexts (Talaván & Rodríguez-Arancón, 2014a). Furthermore, learners' involvement in learning activities is seen on a continuum from teacher-driven learners – who attend a face-to-face, online, or blended course in which the teacher decides how learners can best use ClipFlair – to independent learners, who select and organise their own language learning (Sokoli, 2015; Zabalbeascoa et al., 2012). AVT tasks allow learners to interact with multimodal material that combines verbal (oral and written speech) and non-verbal elements (sound and image) in an innovative way. According to Sokoli (2018), "[m]ultimodal literacy

[…] requires further skills: being able to interpret the multimodal text in its totality, as a complex communication act, and make sense from a combination of verbal and non-verbal sign elements" (p. 80), contrary to the unimodal text approach. In this context, ClipFlair has attempted to develop the traditional four-skill model by proposing the concept of AV skills: AV speaking, AV writing, AV listening and AV reading (Zabalbeascoa et al., 2012). These four AV-specific skills can be defined as follows:

> "[AV speaking and AV writing] refer to the ability to produce speech and writing, respectively, in combination with the video, taking into consideration and adapting to its other elements, such as speed, voice quality, performance, shot transition. […] Similarly, *AV reading* and *AV listening* refer to oral and written comprehension with the combined effect of the elements of the multimodal material" (Sokoli, 2018, p. 80, emphasis in the original).

In order to foster the integration of captioning and revoicing activities in the FL classroom, ClipFlair has created a single online platform – the ClipFlair Studio – where teachers, learners, and activity creators can interact (Baños & Sokoli, 2015). All users can create and access (or modify) ready-made AVT activities in the ClipFlair Studio. Over 400 activities were created within the project framework to help better acquisition of the 15 target languages[9]. To ensure quality, activities were peer-reviewed and tested by project members at different stages and in a number of learning settings. The one-year ClipFlair pilot phase involved more than 1,200 learners, 37 tutors, and 12 languages (Baños & Sokoli, 2015, p. 211). Overall results demonstrate how ClipFlair is appreciated by both learners and teachers. More than 80% of the learners involved in the pilot phase found the activities useful for language learning, and reported that they would like to have such activities in their regular foreign language classroom. The LeViS and ClipFlair projects have created a fruitful environment for teaching-

---

9. The 15 target languages were Arabic, Basque, Catalan, Chinese, English, Estonian, Greek, Irish, Japanese, Polish, Portuguese, Romanian, Russian, Spanish, and Ukrainian. However, activities in other languages, such as Italian and Deutsch, are now available.

oriented research, national, and international collaborations[10], publications and a specific conference on the topic[11]. However, after the end of the ClipFlair project, related research has gradually decreased.

This work focusses on the foreign language classroom, presenting a systematic review of studies carried out in the last twenty years on the applications of captioning and revoicing in this context in order to offer an overview of the state of the art and encourage further research. The literature review will present research on the topic, paying particular attention to relevant experimental studies (i.e. empirical research that involves data collection), which will be reviewed in terms of research focus, target languages, participants, learning settings, audiovisual materials, and captioning/revoicing software and type of analysis (i.e. qualitative and/or quantitative)[12]. The first part will consider studies on captioning, namely on standard interlingual subtitling, reverse interlingual subtitling, and intralingual subtitling. The second part will focus on the research currently available on revoicing: reverse interlingual dubbing, intralingual dubbing, and audio description. Finally, the third part will present the studies that combine captioning and revoicing; in particular, reverse interlingual and intralingual subtitling and dubbing.

---

10. At a national level, in 2010, the National Academy for the Integration of Research, Teaching and Learning (NAIRTL), Ireland, funded the open-ended collaborative website project called Sub2Learn (http://www.sub2learn.ie/) that offers guidelines on how to subtitle, examples of subtitling activities in English, French, and Italian, a list of subtitling software, evaluation guidelines, and a bibliography on subtitles and subtitling in language learning.

11. ClipFlair Conference, Barcelona, 18-19 June 2014 (http://clipflair.net/conference2014/).

12. In quantitative research, data collection procedures provide principally numerical data which is analysed through statistical methods, while in qualitative research data collection procedures mainly aim to present open-ended, non-numerical data which is analysed through non-statistical methods (Dörnyei, 2007). Qualitative and quantitative approaches have become complementary in education research since their combination often results in "findings that may [...] provide a more complete explanation of the research problem than either method alone could provide" (Ary, Cheser Jacobs, & Sorensen, 2009, p. 23).

Captioning

Captioning is the most widely studied AVT mode in foreign language learning. A great number of contributions on pedagogical captioning have been published in the last two decades. The following sections aim to provide an introduction to subtitling and a comprehensive outline of relevant publications and a systematic analysis of experimental studies in the different forms of captioning: standard interlingual subtitling, reverse interlingual subtitling, and intralingual subtitling, respectively.

2.1. Introduction to subtitling

A number of scholars advocate the use of subtitling in language learning. Díaz Cintas (1995, 1997, 2001) foresaw the potential of subtitling in foreign language learning by recognising subtitling as a new and motivating exercise for language learners. He encouraged teachers to incorporate subtitling into their teaching routine since it can enhance vocabulary acquisition and cultural awareness. Subtitling also involves learners in a critical reflection on the linguistic aspects of TV or film products and helps them become acquainted with tools pertaining to much of the professional world in general, such as videos and the PC, which they will most probably use in their future careers.

Although the focus here is on language learning, this type of activity can help raise genuine interest in the professional AVT field among language learners as well. Vermeulen (2003) and Wagener (2006) also suggest the potential of subtitling as a pedagogical tool. Vermeulen proposes subtitling as a motivating exercise for learners thanks to the involvement of video and translation. Focussing on the use of digital laboratories to develop independent learning skills, Wagener presents subtitling as an exploitable resource.

In a greatly-detailed article, Talaván (2006a), proposes the production of standard and reverse interlingual '*ad hoc* subtitles' as a beneficial way of learning an L2 for adolescents and adults of all levels, as "it provides learners with the opportunity to negotiate meaning, to notice language, to become motivated, and to enhance most language learning areas, especially those related to the spoken language, that are typically among the most challenging to teach and acquire" (p. 45). She highlights the active role played by learners in subtitling since it takes place in a motivating context fostered by the multimodal input. The methodological approach respected in Talaván's (2006a) subtitling production proposal is communicative language teaching in combination with task-based learning and teaching. To this regard, Talaván (2010) defines the language learning activities of reading subtitled material[1] and producing subtitles as *subtitles as a support* and *subtitling as a task*, respectively. This precise terminology clearly helps distinguish the two pedagogical applications in language research. Underlining the development of oral comprehension skills, Talaván identifies a number of advantages in applying subtitling, such as the possibility for learners to benefit from authentic multimodal input and to produce a tangible output that can also be shared with peers. Finally, she proposes combining subtitling and subtitles in a single task to create the best impact on foreign language learning.

Talaván (2006b) also anticipates the potential of standard and reverse interlingual subtitling in language for specific purposes education. She presents subtitling as a novel strategy for enhancing the writing and speaking skills of Business English learners, especially in a distant learning context. Learners are required to subtitle short business-related video extracts (from TV series, films, etc.) aimed at definite communicative language functions through *ad hoc* activities. She argues that the subtitling task "has a sense of purpose in itself [...] and the accompanying tasks also look for a sense of communicative achievement that can allow learners to transfer these performance-oriented learning experiences to real life business situations in which they take part" (Talaván, 2006b, p. 327). Furthermore, considering that sociolinguistic and pragmatic competence are

---

1. A great number of studies document the benefits of subtitled videos in language learning and teaching (Gernsbacher, 2015; Vanderplank, 2016). Interestingly, novel forms of subtitled material in foreign language learning are also being studied, such as AV comprehension questions in the form of subtitles (Casañ Núñez, 2017).

fundamental components of Business English learning, the subtitling practice can be particularly effective in fostering speaking skills in this context as it is a valid way to teach spoken English as a foreign language.

Kantz (2015) confirms the effectiveness of interlingual subtitling in language for specific purposes, and in particular regarding English for specific purposes. This scholar describes a study carried out with advanced dentistry students at the *Università degli studi di Pavia*, Italy. After successfully carrying out previous courses proving that multimodal analysis of health-related films are suitable for dentistry students, Kantz (2015) decided to go a step further by asking learners to create the subtitles as well. Divided into four groups, participants collaborated in a virtual learning environment in order to create an annotated corpus of public information films and announcements comprised of sub-corpuses made by each group. The sub-corpus creation involved analysis and classification of the films, selection of the text to be subtitled and, finally, the subtitling of a sample of the sub-corpus. In this context, the term 'subtitle' is used to "include all the metatextual processes that the students wanted to represent" (Kantz, 2015, p. 280). One of the most remarkable outcomes of the study is how learners interpreted the concept of subtitling itself and thus rendered it in different ways, namely interlingual, intralingual, and intertitles (i.e. text placed between film scenes).

Incalcaterra McLoughlin and Lertola (2011) suggest a methodology-based subtitling model while providing a practical example. The authors argue that, far from being a reappraisal of the grammar-translation method, subtitling allows language learners to greatly benefit from translation, which has been reassessed in foreign language learning (Council of Europe, 2001). The translation involved in subtitling implies linguistic and metalinguistic awareness and an ability in contrastive analysis, skills necessary in order to complete a monosemiotic, written translation task as well. Many AV texts lend themselves well to this purpose. In contrast, written translations incorporated in foreign language teaching have often been closed, self-referential systems which exclude the wider linguistic universe that students must perceive and understand when using a foreign language. This shifts focus from a closed, self-referential system to one where there is scope for a wider communicational context, in which non-verbal elements add meaning to each utterance, reinforcing and complementing the verbal element of the communicative act in a foreign language. In audiovisual translation, a communicative reason for the translation (which goes beyond a simple grammatical exercise) is immediately evident, giving a meaningful functional dimension to the new target language text. The authors propose a five-stage methodology-based subtitling model, after testing subtitling activities with Italian B1-level university students of the Bachelor of Arts programme at the National University of Ireland (NUI), Galway. A preparatory stage (which teachers select and prepare the AV material, transcribe the AV dialogue and familiarise themselves with the software), paves the way for five sequential phases, based on a teaching unit model: presentation of the activity (motivation), viewing of the video (global perception), analytical comprehension (analysis), translation-subtitling (synthesis), and considerations on the subtitling process and subtitled clips (reflection). The first phase aims at preparing learners for the activity by increasing their motivation and involvement. This can be done by presenting learners with the AV material to be subtitled by discussing the title and some images taken from the excerpt. In the second phase, learners perceive the communicative situation as a whole. The AV input can be watched a number of times (sound off and sound on respectively) to give the learners the opportunity to familiarise themselves with it and confirm the hypothesis formulated during the discussion in the first phase. Learners can watch the video accompanied by the dialogue transcript in the third phase, and analyse the dialogue by concentrating on the understanding of the message in L2, both in groups and individually. The fourth phase involves metalinguistic considerations since learners are required to translate and subtitle the original spoken dialogue into their L1. The last phase entails a reflection both on language and on the whole learning experience. The model can be used with lower or higher proficiency levels. Similarly, Borghetti (2011) devises the subtitling process in five steps and recommends the subtitling practice expressly for enhancing intercultural education. Foreign language learning gives learners the opportunity to better understand a foreign culture and foster intercultural knowledge. Subtitling proves to be particularly suitable to this purpose since it requires learners to understand an AV foreign language text, which is rich both on a linguistic and a cultural level. The subtitling process for intercultural education is articulated into the following steps: presentation and motivation; viewing; research; synchronisation of subtitles to the video and translating; and editing. Depending on the learning focus – linguistic or intercultural – teachers thus have the opportunity to choose a suitable model to apply in the language learning classroom.

Incalcaterra McLoughlin and Lertola (2014) advocate for the integration of subtitling in the foreign language curriculum. In order to communicate, learners are involved in a number of receptive (aural and visual), productive (oral and written production), interactive (spoken and written interaction), and mediating (oral and written mediation) (Council of Europe, 2001) activities, which can be effectively integrated into a foreign language curriculum. To this end, the authors report an example of such an integration in Italian Studies within the second year of the undergraduate Bachelor of Arts and Bachelor of Commerce degree at NUI, Galway. A subtitling module aimed at teaching the Italian language through the AVT task has been running since September 2008. As an integral part of the core language course, the subtitling module runs for the whole academic year for a total of 24 weeks (one contact hour per week) and contributes to the fulfilment of the general learning objectives of the course, that is allowing undergraduate students to achieve B2 level and preparing them to spend the following year as foreign exchange students in an Italian university. Students are given basic subtitling training and are required to subtitle four short video clips from L2 (Italian) into L1 (English) during the module. Evaluation is obtained through continuous assessment, attendance, and submission of finished subtitles (no final exam is envisaged).

Following the integration of subtitling activities in the foreign language Bachelor degree curriculum, Incalcaterra McLoughlin and Lertola (2015) describe the integration of revoicing and captioning activities through ClipFlair in an online environment. ClipFlair activities are used to date in the Language Lab section in the second year of the Diploma in Italian Online at NUI, Galway, Ireland. The two-year diploma is a part-time course for people interested in learning Italian for professional or personal reasons with no previous knowledge of the language. The aim of the diploma is to achieve A2 level by the end of the first year and B2 by the end of the second. After being trained in intonation reception and production in the first year, learners carry out captioning and revoicing activities in the second year. Video clips used within this framework are carefully selected to fulfil the linguistic content of the syllabus while reinforcing prosodic skills practised during the first year of the course. Learners are asked to provide intralingual subtitles and dub the selected clips; meanwhile, they can discuss their experience in the discussion boards within the course virtual learning environment. As the learners acquire more experience in the required AVT tasks and overcome technical issues, discussions move from learner-teacher to learner-learner. The authors provide five examples of ClipFlair activities in a gradual progression in terms of difficulty. Each activity comprises both captioning and revoicing: reordering intralingual subtitles and then dubbing one character (slow-paced dialogues); inserting verbs in intralingual subtitles and dubbing one/two character(s); inserting vocabulary-keywords and dubbing two characters (individually or in pairs); transcribing intralingual subtitles and recording the script (i.e. subtitles); and writing the script then inserting the subtitles and recording the script. In order to allow learners to focus on language and avoid technical issues while synchronising, the authors suggest to include the timing of the captions in each activity. Although tested in an online learning setting, these activities can also be used in face-to-face contexts.

In the first book devoted to the use of subtitling as a task in language learning, Talaván (2013) significantly contributes to the debate on the integration of AVT in foreign language learning for what concerns both researchers and teachers. After presenting the theoretical framework of subtitling in language learning based on the integration of communicative language teaching and task-based learning and teaching within the guidelines set by the Common European Framework of Reference for languages (Council of Europe, 2001), the author emphasises the crucial role of video in language teaching and learning: AV material provides learners with the unique opportunity to encounter language use in real communicative situations. In the second part of the book, dedicated to the pedagogical potential of subtitling and to its practical applications, the author describes subtitling norms and subtitling software suitable for language teaching and learning. She compares different freeware software and includes very helpful step-by-step guides on how to use subtitling and video editing software. She also presents the limitations of subtitling in foreign language learning, clearly deriving from the author's own extensive first-hand experience. For example, she points to the lack of ready to use materials. Apart from exceptions like the ClipFlair project, which helps solve this issue for several target languages, teachers often have to prepare *ad hoc* activities according to their specific circumstances, which can be greatly time consuming.

Lertola (2015) considers the use of subtitling as a pedagogical tool in the L2 classroom from a teacher's perspective. The author discusses the potential of interlingual and intralingual subtitling in language learning, examining its potential advantages and disadvantages in line with Talaván (2013). The article focusses on how teachers can integrate interlingual subtitling as a language learning task in their teaching routine. To this end, an adaptation of professional subtitling norms for pedagogical purposes is proposed. Learners should be made aware of these basic norms: the subtitling task generally requires a certain amount of translation quality; the translation should respect linguistic and cultural elements of the original dialogue; subtitles should be syntactically and semantically self-contained (distributed on a maximum of two lines). In order to produce effective segmentation of the original dialogue into subtitles, learners should be able to identify sense units in L2. This can prove quite challenging to learners and previous training is encouraged. In addition, it could be useful to provide learners with examples of correct segmentation (e.g. do not split articles or adjectives from nouns, etc.). Bearing in mind that this task is aimed at language learning and not at professional training, Lertola (2015) provides general guidelines for subtitle synchronisation. While synchronising, it could be quite useful to invite learners to employ the professional habit of condensing the message – through partial or total reduction – in order to respect space and time constraints. This practice can also enhance the above-mentioned identification of sense units in L2. Professional linguistic and technical assessment criteria for evaluating learners' subtitled videos are also adapted for language learning purposes. These criteria are divided into five main categories – translation, linguistic, sociolinguistic and pragmatic competence, and technical skills – which are further divided into subcategories. Finally, a description of appropriate

AV material selection is provided, together with a brief record of subtitling tasks suitable for learners with different levels of foreign language proficiency.

Ragni (2018) acknowledges the value of the experimental studies on the pedagogical applications of subtitling, which she defines as 'didactic subtitling', and draws attention to the need for a clearer theoretical framework to support subtitling activities in the foreign language classroom. To this end, she considers a number of theories, from second language acquisition literature and cognitive psychology, that support interlingual subtitling in foreign language learning. After examining how subtitling can be applied within task-based language teaching, she argues for the integration of subtitling and form-focussed instruction. Subtitling is recognised to have specific characteristics that make it an appropriate task to be used in communicative language teaching; however, Ragni (2018) claims that:

> "the subtitling task *alone*, despite the rich and meaningful multimodal environment, may not always result in the internalisation of the [foreign language]. In some cases, therefore, having a more explicit FonFs [Focus on Forms] phase might be necessary. In such a phase, formal instruction is given, language is treated as the object of study rather than communication tool, and students relate themselves to the language as *learners* rather than *users*" (pp. 22-23; emphasis in original).

Although the author provides a few examples, Ragni (2018) does not provide the specifics on how learners' attention can be drawn to linguistic forms after the subtitling task. The author acknowledges that it can be challenging moving from theoretical considerations to real-world applications and encourages further investigation on the topic.

2.2. Standard interlingual subtitling

Research on standard interlingual subtitling is the most developed line of related studies to date, and these experimental studies on standard interlingual subtitling will be discussed in detail in this section. Table 2.1 presents the studies in chronological order by identifying their key features: research focus, target languages, participants, learning settings, AV materials and captioning/revoicing software, and type of analysis (i.e. qualitative and/or quantitative).

Table 2.1. Experimental studies on standard interlingual subtitling in chronological order

Author(s) and date of publication	Research focus	Target languages (from L2 into L1)	Participants[2]	Learning setting	Audiovisual materials	Captioning software	Type of analysis
Bravo, 2008	Idiomatic expression	From English into Portuguese	20 A2/B1-level undergraduate students in Portugal	Face-to-face	Sitcom	Learning via Subtitling	Qualitative and quantitative
Incalcaterra McLoughlin, 2009a	Pragmatic awareness	From Italian into English	10 A1- and 3 B1-level undergraduate students in Ireland	Face-to-face	Movie	Learning via Subtitling	Qualitative
Talaván, 2010, 2011	Listening compre-hension	From English into Spanish	50 A2-level university students in Spain	Face-to-face	Sitcom	Subtitle Workshop	Qualitative and quantitative
Lertola, 2012	Incidental vocabulary acquisition	From Italian into English	16 A2-level university students in Ireland	Face-to-face	Movie	Not specified	Qualitative and quantitative
Borghetti & Lertola, 2014	Intercultural language education	From Italian into English	14 A2/B1-level university students in Ireland	Face-to-face	Movie	Learning via Subtitling	Qualitative
Incalcaterra McLoughlin & Lertola, 2014	Learners' feedback on subtitling	From Italian into English	49 B1/B2-level undergraduate students in Ireland	N/A	N/A	N/A	Qualitative and quantitative

---

2. The language level of the participants is reported only when specifically expressed by the author(s) (i.e. language levels self-assessed by the learners themselves are not considered).

Talaván & Rodríguez-Arancón, 2014a	Listening comprehension	From English into Spanish	10 C1-level university students in Spain	Blended	Movie	ClipFlair	Qualitative and quantitative
Lopriore & Ceruti, 2015	Pragmatic awareness	From English into Italian	19 B1/B2-level postgraduate students in Italy	Blended	Travel documentary	Not specified	Qualitative and quantitative
Incalcaterra McLoughlin & Lertola, 2016	Pragmatic awareness	From Italian into English	20 undergraduate students in Ireland	Face-to-face	Movie	Not specified	Qualitative and quantitative
Lertola, forthcoming	Incidental vocabulary acquisition	From Italian into English	25 A1/A2-level university students in Ireland	Face-to-face	Movie	Learning via Subtitling	Qualitative and quantitative

Bravo (2008) investigates the idiomatic expression retention and recall of 20 Portuguese undergraduate A2/B1 learners of English as a foreign language through subtitling. Students participating in this study were first tested on their familiarity with a number of idiomatic expressions, and results showed that most of them were unfamiliar with these expressions. Students were then exposed to these same idiomatic expressions within AV material (an American sitcom) with intralingual subtitles (L2-L2). They were subsequently asked to recognise these expressions in a multiple-choice post-viewing questionnaire. One week later, students were asked to use the *Learning via Subtitling* simulator to create their own subtitles (from English into Portuguese) for the selected expressions. The students had already carried out one practical session with *Learning via Subtitling* prior to the subtitling task in order to familiarise themselves with the software. Technicalities of subtitling were reduced to a minimum and students only had to subtitle the items under study. In the days following this subtitling activity, students were given the original multiple choice questionnaires on the idiomatic expressions once again. Results showed their knowledge of these expressions had improved (on average nine out of ten expressions were used correctly). Three weeks later, students were provided with a list of paraphrases in Portuguese for each idiomatic expression they had been exposed to in English and were asked to choose seven expressions from the list to include in a coherent written text in English. Students thus had the opportunity to use the newly-acquired English idioms themselves, and the exercise showed very positive results. The majority of the students (15 out of 20) managed to construct coherent and cohesive texts using the seven idioms correctly, while three students used one idiomatic expression wrongly and just two students used two expressions wrongly. This subtitling activity thus proved to highly promote the acquisition of idiomatic expressions. In addition, through repetition of the AV text, students were exposed to the meaning of idiomatic expressions in context, helping to fix these in their memory. An open response questionnaire on the activity showed that students had become more aware of their language competence and subtitling had enhanced their motivation, as they reported that they felt a sense of accomplishment which exceeded their expectations. They had also increased their awareness of cultural differences and lexical structures.

Incalcaterra McLoughlin (2009a) investigates the development of pragmatic awareness in Irish university students of Italian as a foreign language. The level of proficiency of the students involved was diverse: 10 A1, 3 B1 (undergraduate), and 9 C1-C2 (postgraduate). The undergraduate students were attending a regular Italian language course within their degree, while the postgraduates were being trained as translators and interpreters; therefore, the latter will not be considered. Divided into two groups of five ('Group1' and 'Group 2'), the A1 students were all given the same dialogue transcript to translate from L2 (Italian) into L1 (English). Group 1 was then asked to translate the transcription without watching the video clip after being informed about the context of the dialogue. Group 2 was introduced to *Learning via Subtitling* software, asked to watch the video, and create subtitles using the transcription provided. The translations produced by Group 2 demonstrated an attempt to move away from literal translation and a higher degree of pragmatic awareness than those of Group 1. Although considerably more time consuming, subtitling also proved more motivating for students due to "the 'fun' element and the goal of arriving at a meaningful, controllable output" (Incalcaterra McLoughlin, 2009a, p. 232). Group 2 students seemed to better recall lexical elements from the AV dialogue and use more correct syntax three weeks later, when recording some questions for an interview. The three B1 students worked as a single group. These students were shown a scene of an Italian movie, provided with the dialogue transcript and asked to translate it into English. Once translation was complete, they were introduced to *Learning via Subtitling* software and asked to convert the translation into subtitles. As emphasised by Incalcaterra McLoughlin (2009a), the passage from translation into subtitles can raise awareness of underlying linguistic patterns and the semantic value of paralinguistic features. It is therefore preferable to first translate relevant passages rather than to move directly from listening to subtitling. At the end of the subtitling process, students were asked to comment on the differences between their translation and subtitles. When subtitling, besides avoiding literal translation. students indeed seemed to become more aware of some pragmatic features of the text they were translating.

Talaván (2010, 2011) examines the use of subtitling as a task and subtitles as a support in enhancement of listening comprehension skills in a communicative task-based learning context. The quasi-experimental study[3], grounded on two preliminary studies, applied both qualitative and quantitative techniques and involved 50 Spanish adult A2-level learners of English as a foreign language at the Official School of Languages in Spain. Learners were allocated to two groups: experimental and control. Both groups had the same number of participants and were exposed to AV material with intralingual subtitles (L2-L2), but only the experimental group carried out the subtitling activity. Two approximately two-minute video clips of a popular sitcom were selected for the experiment, taking into consideration learners' levels and interests, self-containment of the communicative situation, visual-oral correlation, and the presence of humorous elements. After a preliminary warm-up, all groups watched the first video clip twice with bimodal subtitles. Learners were asked to take notes to test listening comprehension and, after the second viewing, they were asked to summarise the main ideas of the sequence in their L1. Each summary was assessed in terms of 'idea units' which the learners had understood. The experimental group learners were then required to subtitle the first video clip individually in their L1. One of the subtitled clips was chosen at random to be viewed by the whole group as

---

3. A quasi-experimental design generally combines analysis of quantitative and qualitative data, and is often employed in education research in which "the random selection or random assignment of schools and classroom is quite impracticable" (Cohen, Manion, & Morrison, 2007, p. 282).

a finished product. In the meantime, the control group discussed the first video clip and their comprehension of it, giving priority to difficult lexical items. Control group learners watched the clip without subtitles three more times while continuing their discussion. All group work was designed to ensure that the only difference between the groups' experience was the subtitling task performed by the experimental group. Related to the first clip in terms of characters and contexts, the second video clip was shown twice to both groups with intralingual subtitles. The groups again took notes and wrote summaries in L1. A discussion similar to the one previously carried out by the control group was held in both groups as a post-viewing activity. Finally, all learners filled out a self-completion questionnaire containing closed and open questions. Talaván's (2011) concluding statistical analysis of the listening comprehension test confirms the subtitling task as an effective strategy for listening comprehension. Her analysis of both quantitative and qualitative data allows for triangulation[4], providing a higher degree of reliability to the findings of the study.

Lertola (2012) studies the effects of interlingual subtitling tasks on incidental vocabulary acquisition in 16 A2-level undergraduate students of Italian at NUI, Galway. Following a quasi-experimental design, students were divided into two groups: six in the experimental group and ten in the control group. The experimental group carried out a subtitling task from L2 (Italian) into L1 (English) while the control group performed oral comprehension and L2 writing task-based activities on the same video clip. The two groups worked for a total of four hours (one hour per week). During the first hour, both groups completed the same pre-viewing activity that consisted in watching the video twice (the first time with no audio in order to formulate hypotheses, the second with audio in order to confirm or disprove these hypotheses). In the second hour, the experimental group watched the video a third time with a dialogue transcript and worked on comprehension, while the control group watched the video again and carried out oral comprehension task-based activities. The experimental group then performed the subtitling task while the control group carried out oral comprehension and writing tasks in the third and fourth hours.

---

4. Triangulation is usually considered "a valuable and widely used strategy [which] involves the use of multiple sources to enhance the rigour of the research" (Robson, 2002, p. 174).

In order to verify the research hypothesis – whether subtitling results in a more statistically significant retention of new L2 vocabulary – pre, post-immediate and post-delayed vocabulary tests were administered. The pre-test, administered two weeks before the first experimental session, aimed at ensuring that all target words were unknown to the participants. It contained 15 target words and 15 distracters. The immediate and delayed post-tests, administered during the last experimental session and after another two weeks respectively, only included the 15 target words. Findings showed an improvement in learners' incidental acquisition in both groups (though higher in the experimental group). However, statistically significant results emerged at the post-delayed point, proving that subtitling leads to more significant incidental vocabulary acquisition in L2. This small sample does not allow for a generalisation of the results; however, outcomes encourage further investigation.

Borghetti and Lertola (2014) attempt to empirically investigate the application of interlingual subtitling (from Italian into English) for enhancing intercultural language education, based on Borghetti's (2011) work. They report on an exploratory case study carried out at NUI, Galway, with 14 A2/B1-level students of Italian within their regular subtitling module, which is part of their Italian language course (Incalcaterra McLoughlin & Lertola, 2014). Since the study was carried out over a limited amount of time (two weeks), comprehensive development of intercultural competence[5] was not possible. The study thus examines whether the subtitling practice can offer language learners opportunities for cultural and intercultural awareness development. Data was collected through class audio-recordings, initial and final questionnaires, group and pair responses to two teaching forms, semi-structured video-recorded interviews with participants, the teacher's field notes, and students' interlingual subtitles. Results from thematic data analysis reveal that subtitling offers learners "opportunities (possible starting points) for autonomous cultural and intercultural awareness development" (Incalcaterra McLoughlin & Lertola, 2014, p. 436). Although it is mainly the teacher who fosters learners' cultural and intercultural awareness

---

5. According to Byram (2000, in Borghetti, 2011, p. 115) a person possessing a good level of intercultural competence can be defined as "someone who has a critical or analytical understanding of (part of) their own and other cultures – someone who is conscious of their own perspective, of the way in which their thinking is culturally determined, rather than believing that their understanding and perspective is natural" (pp. 117-118).

development through class interaction and discussions, data analysis suggests that even when teacher mediation is limited, subtitling tasks present conditions in which students can better develop their intercultural skills.

Incalcaterra McLoughlin and Lertola (2014) investigate undergraduate students' feedback of the subtitling module integrated in the Bachelor foreign language curriculum through a questionnaire. A total of 49 students attended the subtitling module in four different academic years (2008-2009, 2009-2010, 2010-2011, and 2011-2012), but only 40 completed an online evaluation questionnaire. The six-item questionnaire contains five closed-ended questions and one open-ended question. The first two questions require students to express their agreement or disagreement with four identical statements on subtitling and on translation, if they have also undertaken the latter. Analysis of the responses shows a large majority of learners were happy to see their subtitled product (88%) and were satisfied with it (83%); almost all students (91%) enjoyed the subtitling task. As for the students (32 out of 40) who answered the identical questions about translation, a similar large majority (88%) were happy to see their translation, and were satisfied with it (75%). However, the translation task was enjoyed by 68% of the respondents, therefore to a lesser extent than the subtitling task. In the third question, students rated the improvement they felt they had made (or not) due to subtitling practice in the four traditional language skills – listening, reading, speaking, and writing – as well as in translating, which might be considered as a 'fifth skill' (Colina & Lafford, 2018; Ferreira Gaspar, 2009). Predictably, learners felt they had improved mostly the major skills involved in interlingual standard subtitling, namely translating (93%) and listening (85%). Since the L2 dialogue transcription was used in the subtitling task, more than half of the students (65%) felt they had improved their reading skills. Students had to write the English translation and felt their writing skills (65%) were also enhanced. This confirms Talaván and Rodríguez-Arancón's (2014a) findings in terms of listening comprehension and writing skills. It is also worth noticing that seven out of 49 students were not English native speakers. Therefore, they had translated from L3 (Italian) into L2 (English). Although the subtitling module was mainly presented in Italian and students communicated in L2, the subtitling task did not specifically involve speaking practice. Only a quarter of the students (23%) perceived an improvement in their oral production. For what concerns their AV habits after subtitling, 75% of the students reported that they watch more AV material in a foreign language and most of them (90%) better appreciate subtitled material. Overall, as much as 95% of the students acknowledged that they had enjoyed having subtitling as part of their regular foreign-language course.

Talaván and Rodríguez-Arancón (2014a) investigate the implication of standard interlingual subtitling (from English into Spanish) in the enhancement of listening comprehension skills in advanced English as a foreign language students within a blended learning context at the *Universidad Nacional de Educación a Distancia* (UNED), Spain. Ten C1-level students were asked to subtitle three short video excerpts of a movie using ClipFlair. Students carried out the activities both in the computer labs with the teacher's guidance and assistance, and by themselves at home. Due to the small number of participants, no control group was envisaged. Qualitative and quantitative data was collected through background and final questionnaires, listening comprehension pre- and post-tests, and the teacher's observations in order to apply triangulation and thus provide further reliability. Statistical analysis of the marks obtained in the listening comprehension pre- and post-test show an improvement in learners' performances over one month. These positive results are supported by the learners' opinions in the final questionnaire. The degree of satisfaction regarding the learners' perception of improvement in their listening comprehension is remarkable. Most learners also felt that they had improved their writing skills in the L1. The teacher's observations were direct (face-to-face and by email) and indirect (assessment of the submitted activities). In face-to-face contact, an increase in motivation was observed. For what concerned blended learning, activities were successfully performed autonomously at home. This was also possible thanks to the good information and communication technologies skills of the students involved in the study. As a part of indirect observation, the submitted subtitling activities were assessed using a rubric[6] that included several criteria: accuracy and appropriateness, effectiveness of communication, organisation of the text, and technical aspects.

---

6. A similar rubric, useful for research and teaching purposes, can be found here: http://www.sub2learn.ie/downloads/evaluation_guidelines.pdf

The very positive assessment of the subtitling activities provides further evidence of language learning improvement.

Lopriore and Ceruti (2015) endorse subtitling as a powerful pedagogical tool for pragmatic awareness. Nineteen postgraduate students of a one-year Master course for professional Web, TV, and cinema writers at the *Università di Roma Tre*, Italy, were required to create standard interlingual subtitling samples from English into Italian for six travel documentary excerpts (two to four minutes). This text-type was selected since it is easier to compare to other genres due to the alternation of voice-overs and interviews; it is close to authenticity and it supports understanding through constant oral reference to the images. The subtitling task was accompanied by noticing activities in order to foster pragmatic awareness, such as identifying pragmatic L1 equivalents. Learners were encouraged to motivate their choices and then choose the most suitable equivalent. The authors highlight the importance of individually engaging learners in text comprehension and creation. Data was collected through pre- and post-questionnaires, language tests, and a final interview, allowing for qualitative and quantitative analysis. Comparison of the initial mock-subtitling activities to the final subtitling product clearly shows a greater degree of confidence in providing appropriate L1 equivalents in the final product. One of the unexpected findings of the study was the lack of awareness of pragmatic language features in the L1; apparently, working on the L2 text helped learners to become more aware of the makings of their own native language.

Incalcaterra McLoughlin and Lertola (2016) discuss foreign language learners' attitudes to the translation of impolite language from Italian (L2) to English (L1) within a subtitling task. The study draws from previous research on (im) politeness and the perception of emotional language among non-native speakers; however, it focusses on second language acquisition and the role of AVT in the development of pragmatic awareness and competence in L2. The authors argue that reflection on the perceived emotional impact of swearwords and other taboo or vulgar expressions in translation can help to enhance students' ability to communicate appropriately in a given context. In particular, AVT can be extremely beneficial to this aim, since the texts learners are asked to work with provide examples of communication in realistic situations presented in an AV product. Clearly, filmic language differs from spontaneous conversation, and a number of stylistic choices inform the construction of film dialogue. However, AV dialogue proves particularly useful in language education (Pavesi, 2012), especially in the context of foreign (as opposed to second) language learning where spontaneous input is more limited and often constrained by the formality of classroom interaction. In line with previous research illustrating the higher impact of swearwords in one's native language, the study suggests that learners provide a weaker translation of impoliteness in their L1 compared to the original L2 text. The empirical study compares the collaborative translation of five native English speakers with the individual translations of 11 native English speakers, and those of four non-native English speakers[7] at NUI, Galway, Ireland. The study shows that the percentage of impolite language translated by learners is generally high (69%, 72%, and 81% for the three groups, respectively). However, the strength of the impolite language used varies. Learners from the non-native speakers group, working from L3 to L2, were more willing to employ stronger expressions, suggesting that swearwords had a lower impact on them. Since the offensiveness of a word is determined by pragmatic variables such as the identity of the speaker/listener, their relationship and social norm, future research should involve a larger number of participants from different age groups, sexes, and levels of proficiency, working both individually and together in different language learning contexts.

Lertola (forthcoming) investigates the role of subtitling tasks on incidental vocabulary acquisition in 25 A1-A2 native-English speaking undergraduate students of Italian at NUI, Galway, after extensive piloting (Lertola, 2012). The author concludes that subtitling engages learners in complex information processing involving both acoustic and video channels. Considering that noticing is an essential aspect of language acquisition, she also reasons that subtitling tasks facilitate learners in noticing L2 words due to contrastive association with their L1 equivalent. In particular, Laufer and Hulstijn's (2001) *involvement load hypothesis* for vocabulary acquisition postulates that tasks are more effective if they imply

---

7. One French, two German, one Portuguese, and one Spanish student.

a greater involvement load, which combines three factors – need, search, and evaluation – with regard to the words. Lertola (forthcoming) argues that:

> "the subtitling task can be considered as task-induced involvement since it simultaneously implies need, search and evaluation. Need, the motivational dimension of the involvement, is present in the task when a word is necessary for comprehension. To subtitle, learners are required to achieve a good understanding of the foreign-language text and thus they experience the need to understand unknown words. Search and evaluation represent the cognitive dimension of involvement. Search takes place when learners are looking for the meaning of a new L2 word or for the L2 form. Learners then experience evaluation when choosing the appropriate meaning of a word in its context. For instance, if a word has more than one meaning, learners must select the one which best applies to the context".

The study followed a mixed research design (combining qualitative and quantitative data collection and analysis). Due to the restricted number of participants, four types of triangulation were employed, namely data, observer, methodological, and theory. Quantitative data was collected through vocabulary pre- and immediate post-tests. Qualitative data offering valuable understanding thus allowing for better interpretation of the findings was also collected through an initial questionnaire that informed on participants' background information as well as their AV habits and preferences, a final questionnaire which provided participants' feedback, classroom audio, and video recordings, and classroom observations. The results of the study, obtained through statistical analysis, show that interlingual subtitling promotes the incidental acquisition of new word meanings in terms of productive recall.

2.3. Reverse interlingual subtitling

Reverse interlingual subtitling is gradually gaining scholars' attention, particularly with regard to writing skills. Relevant studies will be presented in this section and can be seen in Table 2.2. Similarly to Table 2.1, Table 2.2 shows a chronologically-ordered overview of studies on reverse interlingual subtitling organised by their key characteristics – research focus, target languages, participants, learning settings, AV materials, captioning/revoicing software, and type of analysis.

Table 2.2. Experimental studies on reverse interlingual subtitling in chronological order

Author(s) and date of publication	Research focus	Target languages (from L1 into L2)	Participants	Learning setting	Audiovisual material	Captioning software	Type of analysis
Talaván & Rodríguez-Arancón, 2014b	Writing and translation skills	From Spanish into English	40 B1-level undergraduate students in Spain	Online	Movie	Aegisub	Qualitative and quantitative
Burczyńska, 2015	Writing skills	From Polish into English	24 students of a foreign language school in Poland	Face-to-face	Movie	Subtitle Workshop	Qualitative and quantitative
Talaván, Ibáñez, & Bárcena, 2016a	Writing skills	From Spanish into English	68 undergraduate students in Spain	Online	Movie	Aegisub	Qualitative and quantitative

Talaván and Rodríguez-Arancón (2014b) explore whether reverse subtitling as a collaborative language learning tool can develop writing and translation skills in a distance learning context. A total of 40 undergraduate students of English (level B1) at UNED were involved in the experimental study and were equally divided into experimental and control groups. Participants in the experimental group were further divided into four groups and were required to provide English subtitles for two video clips of a Spanish movie working collaboratively online over two and a half months. Collaborative work was fostered by the use of the university virtual learning environment through forums, chat rooms, and video conferencing. In the meantime, control group participants performed noncollaborative student-centred online activities that did not comprise subtitling. The study provides data through pre- and post-questionnaires, writing and translation assessment tests, and teachers' observations. Two observers also assessed the language tests following specific rubrics with specific evaluation criteria. The criteria for assessment of the writing assignment included clarity, focus, coherence development, knowledge, critical thinking, intellectual ambition, expression, grammar and usage, and academic conventions. The criteria for assessing the translation tests were accuracy and appropriateness of the translated text, grammatical/syntactic constructions, good use of vocabulary, organisation of text, cohesion and coherence, and effectiveness of communication. The average mark of writing and translation tests from pre- and post-test shows an improvement both in writing and translation skills for the two groups. However, improvement in the experimental group is higher than in the control group (0,7 and 1,2 in the writing and translation tests respectively). These results are also backed up by post-questionnaire answers. Learners' perceptions of writing and translation skills development was particularly high, especially in the experimental group. General satisfaction with regard to written production and translation competence was also confirmed by teachers' observations. The collaborative work was also perceived as beneficial by most learners; particularly in terms of written expression, vocabulary acquisition, use-of-English confidence, and grammar knowledge. Overall findings seem to confirm that reverse subtitling can be used as a beneficial activity for L2 writing and translation.

Burczyńska (2015) presents a pilot study with 24 Polish learners of English at a foreign language school in Poland. Here too, the students were evenly divided into an experimental and a control group. For the specific context of creating reverse subtitles in the foreign language class, the author proposes an adaptation of Neves's (2004) framework of subtitling process, followed in translator training. Data collected through pre- and post-questionnaires, interviews (with a limited number of participants), and written assignments are analysed qualitatively and quantitatively. Two months after the pilot, participants in the experimental group made fewer grammar mistakes and fewer spelling mistakes compared to the control group in the post-written assignment. As suggested by post-questionnaire answers, learners also perceived an improvement in their vocabulary, including fixed expressions and idioms. In addition, when interviewed, experimental group participants acknowledged finding the subtitling activity "a thought provoking, simulated task" (Burczyńska, 2015, p. 239). All participants were eager to have these types of activities in their regular foreign language class. The author calls for an integration of subtitling in the regular foreign language course both for writing and vocabulary enhancement.

Talaván et al. (2016a) investigate collaborative reverse subtitling for the enhancement of written production activities in an online setting within a research project on *Collaborative AVT to Improve Language Skills* in English as a second language at UNED, Spain. The month and a half mixed-research experimental study involved 68 undergraduate students of English who were divided into two equal groups (experimental and control). The experimental group participants, divided into sub-groups, had to subtitle two excerpts of a Spanish comedy into English. Each sub-group had to agree on a draft translation of the subtitles, and each member had to add subtitles to each video and share these with other members. Finally, the sub-group was asked to choose the most linguistically and technically accurate subtitled version of the two movie excerpts among the members' videos. The data collection tools were initial and final questionnaires, pre- and post- writing production tests, and teacher's observations. The language assessment tests required participants to write two essays and were evaluated following an *ad hoc* rubric compiled by two of the teachers involved in the project. In order to reach a higher degree of reliability, the quantitative analysis made use of correlation studies and distribution of average marks of the tests. Improvement was detected in both groups. However, a greater degree of improvement was found in the experimental group. According to the authors (Talaván et al., 2016a), "the learning experience has influenced writing skills development in the [experimental group], while the [control group] members have improved at a slower pace, [...] there is a direct cause-effect relationship between the reverse subtitling process and the improvement of written production" (p. 12). For what concerns participants' perception, subtitling was identified as useful for a number of factors rated in the following order: material authenticity, activity creativity, and technology-based settings including both subtitling software and virtual learning environment tools (like chats and forums). The collaborative nature of the project was positively evaluated by participants. In particular, they appreciated the opportunity to evaluate and discuss with peers, their assessment obtained from peers, and the teachers' supervision. Teachers' observations confirm the participants' commitments to the project and their effort in working together. Considering their experience in previous distance-learning projects, the authors appraise collaborative reverse subtitling as especially motivating for English as a second language learners.

2.4. Intralingual subtitling

Investigation on the application of intralingual subtitling in foreign language classrooms is quite limited. However, two such studies have been identified. One was carried out by López Cirugeda and Sánchez Ruiz (2013) combined with revoicing and will thus be considered in Chapter 4, *Combined captioning and revoicing*. The other study by Talaván, Lertola, and Costal (2016b) will be presented here; its main features are shown in Table 2.3.

Table 2.3. Experimental studies on intralingual subtitling in chronological order

Author(s) and date of publication	Research focus	Target languages (from L2 into L2)	Participants	Learning setting	Audiovisual material	Captioning software	Type of analysis
Talaván et al., 2016b	Writing skills and incidental vocabulary acquisition	From English into English	41 B1-level undergraduate students in Spain	Online	Sitcom	ClipFlair	Qualitative and quantitative

Talaván et al. (2016b) present the findings of a study on intralingual captioning (iCap) for the enhancement of writing skills and vocabulary acquisition. The study was carried out with 41 B1-level undergraduate students of English at

UNED, Spain over a month and a half in a distance-learning setting. Participants were asked to provide intralingual subtitles – not a simple transcription of the original dialogue but a condensed version of the spoken text – to ten excerpts of an American sitcom using ClipFlair. According to the authors, when creating intralingual subtitles, learners can foster their written production since they have to pay attention to register and style, cohesion and coherence, as well as spelling. As regards vocabulary learning, while subtitling, students are asked to listen carefully to the original dialogue and identify new L2 words in order to understand the message; then, they should rephrase the text to condense the message so as to respect time and space constraints. Quantitative and qualitative data was gathered through initial and final questionnaires, writing, and vocabulary pre-tests and post-tests, and observation, thus allowing for triangulation. Two observers assessed the writing pre- and post-tests in which students were required to produce two approximately 150 word essays in 60 minutes. The *ad hoc* evaluation rubric included five assessment criteria (readability, coherence, cohesion, length, and general impression) that were evaluated considering B1-level written production. The vocabulary pre-test, aimed at measuring the productive recall of meaning, was comprised of 50 target words selected in ten video excerpts belonging to the *Corpus of Contemporary American English-Academic*, plus 25 distracters. Students taking the pre-test did not know that they were going to be tested again. The vocabulary post-test only contained the 50 target words. As for vocabulary tests, it should be noted that target words were selected on the basis of 70 participants, the initial total number which was ultimately reduced to 41, since dropout rate can be quite high in online learning contexts. Quantitative analysis was carried out with a subgroup of participants and target words; it thus does not provide generalisable conclusions. However, qualitative analysis supports learners' perceptions of an improvement in their vocabulary knowledge. Data analysis of the writing tests provides evidence of the benefits produced by intralingual subtitling on written production, backed up by answers, a final questionnaire, and researchers' observations.

Revoicing

Revoicing in foreign language learning is gradually gaining scholars' attention. A number of contributions on the benefits of L2 revoicing tasks have been published in the last 20 years. Within revoicing, dubbing has been the most studied AVT technique[1]; however, audio description has started to be considered as an effective task in the foreign language classroom. Recently, voice-over has also raised interest among researchers proving its potential in language learning. The following sections aim to provide a comprehensive outline of many important publications which make up this area of research followed by a systematic analysis of experimental studies on dubbing, AD, and voice-over respectively.

3.1. Dubbing

One of the first proposals to introduce dubbing as a language learning activity dates as far back as to the late Eighties. Within a more ample discussion on the use of translation, Duff (1989) argues that dubbing as 'applied translation' could enhance language production and peer-to-peer collaboration. The dubbing task he describes requires learners to translate a theatre play for a movie version and read it aloud, respecting the idiomatic expressions and initial cultural references.

While advocating for the use of translation as an effective communicative tool in teaching English as a foreign language, Zohrevandi (1994) proposes collaboratively dubbing a movie or a play from English into L1 together with other activities for enhancing listening and speaking skills. The author recommends dividing the class into pairs or groups, showing learners a movie or play (maximum duration of about 45 minutes) or asking them to watch it at

---

1. Similarly to subtitling, dubbing has been considered as a teaching tool both in the language classroom and in translators' training (Barbe, 1996; Jüngst, 2013). However, it goes beyond the scope of this work to examine this second aspect.

home. Each learner transcribes the assigned part to be dubbed individually to foster listening skills, and then translates it into L1. The individual translations are combined in order to have the complete dubbing script ready to be practiced and performed, thus also promoting oral production. Such an activity could be carried out with teacher guidance or individually outside the classroom context.

Kumai (1996) relates his three-year experience on using dubbing to improve phonetic competence in the English as a foreign language classroom. In particular, he claims that dubbing movies provides learners with the opportunity to improve pronunciation, intonation, and speed through reproducing native speakers' utterances. Giving learners the chance to select which movie and which excerpt of the movie to dub – combined with a public presentation of the dubbed product – contributes to making the activity especially motivating.

Burston (2005) confirms the motivational value of dubbing sound-off video clips. Besides the novelty of the activity, dubbing can be less intimidating to learners than live performances. With regards to pedagogical aspects, the author answers a simple but essential question:

> "what is to be gained through [dubbing] that could not just as well (and more easily) be accomplished by traditional role play activities? One important difference is the nature of the potential audience and the effect the audience can have upon student performance. […] The [dubbed] finished product can not only be shown in class but also, if the means exist to do so, put up on a course web site for all to see. The greater the audience, the greater the stimulus to put on a good public performance" (Burston, 2005, p. 80).

According to the author, a further advantage of dubbing compared to role plays is that dubbing "can be done and redone as often as needed to get the best possible final results. Students can self-monitor and improve their oral performance in a way that is just not possible in real time" (Burston, 2005, p. 80). Students must also respect time constraints in order to produce lyp-synchronised speech, thus fostering speed.

Burston (2005) identifies two dubbing options with different degrees of difficulty. The easiest option, 'simple video dubbing', consists in substituting the original soundtrack with students' voices; more advanced students (or those with previous dubbing experience) can prepare their own storyline and script for a muted video, a technique defined as 'scenario creation'. The first option allows learners mainly to improve listening and speaking skills. Apart from oral production, the second option can also enhance reading and writing skills as well as grammar and vocabulary knowledge. In this way, dubbing provides similar pedagogical benefits to video making but proves less complex in terms of classroom time and logistics. However, it still requires preparation, especially in technical terms, both for teachers and learners.

After presenting the ClipFlair project, Navarrete (2013) describes a dubbing-based experience in a Spanish as a foreign language classroom. The workshop 'Lend your voice to an actor' was carried out with 20 A1-level secondary school students of Spanish from different classes in England. The workshop had been organised by Imperial College London and Routes into Languages[2] as a first exposure to intralingual dubbing in the classroom and a way to test dubbing tasks for the ClipFlair project. The dubbing task did not involve translation; students were asked to order the dialogue that was presented to them in a scrambled order, and then dub the video excerpt of a Spanish TV series by replicating the original dialogues over one hour and 45 minutes. The workshop was divided into two parts: the first focussed on the presentation of the video excerpt and its listening comprehension through a number of tasks (including order of the dialogue), and the second aimed at making students familiar with ClipFlair and dubbing itself, and at creating a group reflection on the experience. The dubbing task proved to be highly motivating, as suggested by Kumai (1996) and Burston (2005), and allowed for greater language and intercultural awareness. However, from a practical point of view, a greater amount of time allotted for carrying out the activity would have been beneficial. In conclusion, the author insists on the importance of video selection for the success of the dubbing task.

---

2. https://www.routesintolanguages.ac.uk/

Wakefield (2014) compares dubbing with traditional acting[3]. While identifying the advantages and limitations of dubbing compared to traditional drama techniques, the author states that:

> "there is one key aspect for which dubbing arguably has an advantage over traditional forms of acting. [...] Dubbing allows learners to make all of the choices regarding genre, vocabulary, proficiency level, because they can select from among the virtually limitless number of easily accessible online videos. Play scripts can also be adapted by students, but not all learners are able and willing to create or modify scripts" (Wakefield, 2014, p. 160).

Wakefield (2014) also suggests that dubbing practice can be employed as an additional drama technique or as a preparation exercise before carrying out live drama performances. To this regard, dubbing can be used quite advantageously as a self-learning task. In addition, it can prove especially beneficial to shy learners that may fear stage performance since the audience, if any, focusses on the video rather than on the learner. Besides providing practical guidelines for teachers on how to prepare a dubbing task, the author proposes letting learners listen to the L2 dialogue in order to learn it and dub it. Learners might also write the L2 dialogue and look up unknown words. This additional vocabulary exercise can prove to be challenging and, in some cases, requires the help of a native speaker. Nevertheless, memorising and acting out L2 dialogues can be beneficial both for fluency and proficiency in the target language.

González Davies (2004) proposes dubbing as a way for intermediate and advanced students to become more aware of different options in translation and overcome limitations among the various activities highlighted in her book, *Multiple Voices in the Translation Classroom*. The book is addressed "to translation trainers and students, and also to foreign language teachers who wish to include translation activities in a communicative and interactive way in their

---

3. Maley and Duff (2005) describe in detail drama techniques to be used as communication activities in the language classroom. Drama techniques can foster integrated language skills, motivation, self-awareness, and awareness of the others as well as self-esteem and confidence. The voice plays a key role in drama activities; to this end, a number of activities are suggested to prepare and carry out voicework.

classrooms" (González Davies, 2004, p. 6). The author suggests that dubbing activities be carried out in the following three steps.

- The students receive the source text of an extract from a film and translate it.

- They compare their translations with those of other students.

- Finally, they listen to the dubbed version and compare [their own version to that of] professional dubbers [discussing and justifying] their own choices (González Davies, 2004, p. 181).

As can be noticed, no actual revoicing is involved since the core activity in this dubbing exercise is translation, and comparison with versions produced by peers and professionals. In this case, learners can benefit from the standard or reverse translation of the original dialogue. Instead, in his book on dialogue activities, Bilbrough (2007) recommends setting up a class dubbing project to enhance spoken interaction. The focus of his project is to raise awareness in pre-intermediate language learners of their English proficiency. To this end, learners are given the dialogue script of an excerpt from a movie or a soap opera, and are asked to dub the lines on to the silent clip in about 20 minutes. The teacher should assist learners while rehearsing the lines to foster text understanding and pronunciation. After the groups of students have dubbed the silent excerpt, their versions may be shown to the class, followed by the excerpts with the original voices. The teacher should then encourage learners' considerations on their performances.

Bilbrough (2007) also provides three variations of the project. In order to foster listening and writing skills, the first variation suggests not giving the script to the learners and, after playing the excerpts, asking them to write the script as they can remember it and, ultimately, to dub the excerpt. A comparison with the original version and students' performance is encouraged. The second variation consists in giving learners the original scene dialogue translated by the instructor into L1 before watching the original video, so that they can translate it into L2, and dub their version onto the excerpt. The last variation considers showing learners a scene in L1 and asking them to provide the L2 version to be dubbed on to the video.

Yachi and Karimata (2008) present Act Inside the Video Environment (ActIVE), a web application that allows language learners to dub videos. The videos available on the system are short clips featuring common situations (a chat with friends, business meetings, or conversations between salespeople) in the learners' mother tongue or another known language, so that learners can understand the scene and play their roles accordingly. In order to avoid word-for-word translation, the scene duration is fixed. Learners must therefore identify the core message and provide a translation that respects time constraints. To do so, they can practice their lines as much as they want, before making the final recording. The web application allows two learners to work at the same time. A pilot study to test the web platform was carried out with learners of English in a Japanese university. Although proving to be a user-friendly system, findings from the pilot study suggest that technological adjustments are needed.

Shevchenko and Blanco-Arnejo (2005) describe the steps necessary for technology-enhanced student projects which involve dubbing into L2, along with the rationale behind these projects. They argue that these projects are both motivating and empowering, since they require learners to "negotiate meaning through interaction, interpretation, and collaboration" (Shevchenko & Blanco-Arnejo, 2005, cited in Danan, 2010, p. 446) while dealing with cultural and linguistic nuances. Finally, given the increase of language teaching in digital environments and the pedagogical potential of video, Wagener (2006) reports on pilot research on the use of digital laboratories to develop independent learning skills, and presents dubbing among the exploitable resources of digital video. The pilot activity which includes dubbing was carried out within a German third year module in translation and was related to the improvements in consecutive translation. However, it is not specified whether the module was part of a more general translator-training degree.

Talaván (2013) advocates for the integration of revoicing, dubbing and AD in particular, in foreign language curriculums. After describing various revoicing tasks and how they can benefit language learning, the author offers examples of such tasks that can be easily employed in face-to-face, blended, or classroom contexts. Furthermore, based on hands-on experience, Talaván (2013) presents an *ad hoc* rubric for assessing dubbing projects.

3.1.1. Reverse interlingual dubbing

Experimental research on reverse interlingual dubbing – the oral translation of the original L1 spoken dialogue into L2 – seems to be quite limited, as can be seen in Table 3.1.

Table 3.1. Experimental studies on reverse interlingual dubbing in chronological order

Author(s) and date of publication	Research focus	Target languages (from L1 into L2)	Participants	Learning setting	Audiovisual material	Captioning software	Type of analysis
Danan, 2010	Speaking and writing skills	From English into Dari, Pashto or Farsi	82 Army students in the United States	Face-to-face	TV series, movies and animated cartoons	Windows Movie Maker, iPod	Qualitative

Danan (2010) provides one of the first more comprehensive insights on dubbing in language learning, since she proposes a theoretical framework for integrating AVT into task-based instruction and describes a series of exploratory reverse dubbing projects. She highlights the communicative aspects of translation and reviews the recent revaluation of translation as a meaningful pedagogical tool. These considerations can be extended to AVT. Contrary to subtitles as a support, Danan (2010) notices that very little has been published on the use of dubbed videos in language learning[4]. The standard

---

4. To fill this gap, Ghia and Pavesi (2016) investigate the potential of the language of dubbing in L2 learners-viewers. Starting from the assumption that – as the outcome of a translation process – dubbed dialogues are subject to translation universals (such as simplification, explicitation, and standardisation), the authors hypothesise that these strategies can benefit accessibility and, ultimately, language acquisition. Results from their study show that dubbed input results in better comprehension compared to non-translated film dialogue, independently of the L1 of viewers and individual features of audiovisual texts.

dubbed version usually presents the L1 spoken dialogue, which has substituted the L2 original. She recalls a number of Italian studies on students' contrastive analysis of dubbed versions of English movies. Such comparative analyses can foster pragmatic language awareness in advanced students. Danan's (2010) study involved American Army learners of Dari, Pashto, or Farsi engaged in an intensive language programme over one year. A total of 82 students undertook 15 dubbing projects over three years, some of these were teacher-led at first and others were entirely student-led. The aim of these dubbing projects was to give learners an opportunity to vary the six-hour per day intensive programme and to promote peer-to-peer collaboration as well as participation. The public presentation of the dubbed projects to other classmates and teachers was also seen as a stimulus. Most of all, the dubbing task aimed at enhancing skill integration – written and spoken production – though authentic communicative language use.

Learners were required to translate the original L1 dialogue of either TV series, English-language films, or animated cartoon excerpts into L2 providing a culturally appropriate equivalent which demonstrated an awareness of register and was adapted to the communicative situation. Learners usually had to resort to more colloquial speech than in everyday classroom discourse, and in a concise way in order to respect time constraints. Beyond this, "they had the challenge of delivering their lines with an emphasis on fluency and speed, correct pronunciation and intonation, while incorporating paralinguistic elements into their delivery to act out emotions (anger, surprise, fear, etc.)" (Danan, 2010, p. 447). Students' feedback obtained through post-project questionnaires confirmed that dubbing had enhanced their vocabulary acquisition, speaking production (fluency, pronunciation, and expressiveness), and motivation.

Although dubbing projects were a compulsory assignment and proved to be quite time consuming, the majority of the students found dubbing a stimulating and enjoyable group activity. Interestingly, Danan (2010) reports that

> "[s]tudent-initiated projects were indeed most successful in terms of commitment to the work and enthusiasm among all the participants. But

entirely student-led projects in which teachers had little involvement resulted in uncorrected mistakes, whereas grammar, vocabulary, and pronunciation accuracy was the highest when teachers were closely engaged in the various stages" (p. 453).

The author suggests that a happy medium between teacher control and student initiative could be reached by empowering learners through periodical guidance and feedback so as to attain ideal language learning conditions (Danan, 2010). To this regard, she also recommends monitoring learners' progress at different stages by, for instance, making a review of the translation with the entire class, providing after-class coaching, and encouraging the production of mock recording exercises at home in order to receive pronunciation and grammar feedback before final voice recordings.

3.1.2. Intralingual dubbing

Contrary to reverse interlingual dubbing, there are a number of experimental studies on intralingual dubbing (the voice repetition of the original spoken language), as shown in Table 3.2. Most of the studies involve English as a target language in face-to-face university contexts.

Table 3.2. Experimental studies on intralingual dubbing in chronological order

Author(s) and date of publication	Research focus	Target language (from L2 into L2)	Participants	Learning setting	Audiovisual material	Captioning software	Type of analysis
Chiu, 2012	Speaking skills	English	83 undergraduate students in Taiwan	Face-to-face	Movie or TV series	N/A	Qualitative and quantitative
He & Wasuntarasophit, 2015	Speaking skills	English	34 students in China	Face-to-face	TV series	Not specified	Qualitative and quantitative

Florente, 2016	Speaking skills	English	Seven university students in China	Face-to-face	Movie	Not specified	Qualitative
Sánchez Requena, 2016	Speaking skills	Spanish	20 B1/B2-level secondary-school students in England	Face-to-face	TV series	Windows Movie Maker	Qualitative
Talaván & Costal, 2017	Speaking skills and assessment guidelines	English	B2-level university students in Spain	Online	Sitcom	ClipFlair	Qualitative and quantitative
Sánchez Requena, 2018	Speaking skills	Spanish	47 B1-level secondary-school students in England	Face-to-face	Short movies, TV series and programmes	Not specified	Qualitative and quantitative

Chiu (2012) investigates how dubbing can enhance oral production in English as a foreign language conversation classes. According to the author, "[t]he method of film dubbing offers a unique opportunity for the imitation of English pronunciation and intonation within a contextualised scenario" (Chiu, 2012, p. E24). She carried out an experiment with 83 undergraduate students in an urban college in Northern Taiwan who had been introduced to basic English-pronunciation rules in a previous one-year course. The students were divided into two groups: 41 students in the experimental group (Group A), and 42 in the control group (Group B). Group A performed the dubbing task, while Group B attended a conversation course. Group A participants were further divided into subgroups of two to four people. Each group had to select a ten-minute clip from a movie or TV series, and dub the clip in front of the class as a final exam by reading the muted-video's subtitles. In view of the exam, after rehearsing their lines, students had to watch the entire movie to "ensure that they could put the correct emotion to the film" (Chiu, 2012, p. E25). Data collection instruments consisted in a questionnaire and semi-structured interviews. Quantitative analysis of the questionnaire shows that Group A outperformed Group B. The semi-structured interviews, whose coding was cross-checked by an independent observer, provide qualitative findings that back up the quantitative results. Dubbing helped learners reduce mispronunciation, improving their fluency and intonation awareness. However, the author observes that it is not clear from the data whether learners made noticeable improvements in fluency, delivery and pronunciation, nor is the extent to which they made obvious progress evident. Therefore, further research is needed in this regard. Talaván and Costal (2017) recommend making several adaptations before carrying out a second repetition: the clips should be between one and two minutes in duration, and for the task to be classified as dubbing, actual recordings ought to take place.

He and Wasuntarasophit (2015) investigate the outcomes of dubbing on improving oral proficiency with 34 Chinese English as a foreign language learners who were asked to dub a 26-minute episode of an American TV series over four weeks. Students were provided with English scripts, and the video was both English captioned and Chinese subtitled. Given that elsewhere dubbing a 20-minute TV series episode took students 20 hours (Danan, 2010), students were encouraged to work one hour per day during the four weeks of the project as the dubbing task was an after-class assignment. Two spontaneous speaking pre- and post-tests were administered in order to measure students' progress. Test results show that students' oral proficiency (in terms of comprehensibility, fluency, and accent) improved. Students' attitudes toward the task were also analysed by means of a questionnaire and an interview. Although the dubbing was considered a challenging task, the students' overall attitude towards this revoicing technique was positive to the point that some of them were eager to continue dubbing. Valuable suggestions were also provided by the participants: they suggested using a shorter video with a lower speech rate and obtaining more constant feedback from the teacher.

Florente (2016) investigates whether the use of movie scripts and dubbing activities increases awareness of prosodic features in English – specifically, awareness of sentence stress – in Chinese learners of English as a foreign language. The author reports on the findings from a qualitative study with seven second-year English students (in a classroom of 28 people) at a university in Beijing, China. After being briefly introduced to word and sentence stress both at practical and theoretical levels, students were involved in three cycles of spoken-dialogue listening activities. They were required to record their answers to pronunciation questions and dub a movie clip. Activities and questionnaire responses were gathered and analysed to determine whether students' sentence-stress awareness had developed after these three cycles of language instruction. The *ad hoc* rubric used for assessing dubbing contained three criteria: intonation, sentence stress, and overall intelligibility. The dubbing task scores were generally high, and results show that the ability of most students to perceive sentence stress was better than their theoretical awareness of it. However, many students made pronunciation errors of certain vowels, and showed a lack of intonation. The author suggests that pronunciation could have been improved with more practice before the final dubbing. In addition, students' comments underlined the importance of reproducing emotions in order to perform dubbing correctly, as pointed out by Chiu (2012).

Sánchez Requena (2016) reports on a pilot study focussed on the development of fluency and pronunciation in spontaneous conversations through intralingual dubbing. The pilot study involved 20 B1/B2-level secondary-school learners of Spanish in England. Learners were required to dub a total of nine videos from a Spanish TV series over six weeks using Windows Movie Maker. The teacher had previously subtitled the short videos – including the exact transcription of the dialogues – using Subtitle Workshop. Mainly qualitative data was gathered through individual interviews, two questionnaires, and the teacher's notes. Learners were interviewed individually about general topics using different tenses for 20 minutes before and after the dubbing activity. Only the most representative four-minute samples of the interviews were considered for both quantitative and qualitative analysis. In quantitative analysis, words per minute were calculated before and after, showing an average improvement of approximately 22 words per minute. As for qualitative analysis, three Spanish native speakers and teachers of Spanish as an L2 examined the interviews in terms of fluency and pronunciation.

The most noteworthy improvements were identified in self-correction, fast-paced communication, and spontaneity. Pauses and hesitations decreased considerably after the dubbing task. The preliminary results were also confirmed by the questionnaire responses. The three native speakers also detected small improvements in pronunciation. The author suggests that more explicit instructions should be given on pronunciation in order to obtain more significant advances. The first questionnaire administered both before and after dubbing shows that students' perception of their Spanish spoken production improved. The second questionnaire gathered students' feedback about the general use of AVT in the classroom, and more specifically about their dubbing experience. Students felt they had mostly improved their oral skills, followed by listening. Reading and writing skills were also enhanced according to the students. Interestingly, vocabulary acquisition and grammar were the areas learners felt they had developed the most and the least respectively. Finally, the teacher's notes were taken observing the students during the contact hours and while listening to the dubbed products.

These notes identified a number of advantages offered by dubbing, as follows.

- It provides the student with a realistic idea of speed in native dialogues.

- It offers more knowledge of the Spanish culture as [students] can observe it for themselves.

- It facilitates [acquisition] of new vocabulary and colloquial expressions.

- It encourages the development of fluency and pronunciation.

- It increases confidence when expressing orally.

- It is a motivating activity.

- It is seen as a fun and different activity.

- [Students become more aware of their own learning processes] as they can listen to themselves and self-assess.

- Students notice improvement in their pronunciation, intonation, and speed when communicating.

- Indirectly, students notice improvement in their listening comprehension (Sánchez Requena, 2016, p. 18).

A number of limitations – seen as helpful feedback in view of future research – are also mentioned.

- Subtitles are not always easy to read.

- In some occasions, an excessive difficulty of some clips can discourage students.

- Sometimes, pronunciation and intonation is sacrificed due to the large quantity of continuous speech.

- Excessive speed and length of some videos could make students feel that they have not improved in any skill.

- Not all the topics were as engaging (some topics were more interesting for the participants) (Sánchez Requena, 2016, p. 18).

It should be noted that the advantages of dubbing outnumber its limitations, and these field-experience suggestions can be of use to scholars and teachers who wish to employ intralingual dubbing in the foreign language classroom.

Sánchez Requena (2018) continues her research on the benefits of intralingual dubbing on oral production skills, focussing in particular on pronunciation, intonation, and speed. Apart from examining such benefits, another aim of her contribution is to collect useful feedback to serve as a guide on how to employ dubbing in the Spanish as a foreign language classroom in order to facilitate the teaching practice. The author carried out an experimental study with 47 B1-level students learning Spanish in five different secondary schools in England. The students were asked to dub nine one-minute-long Spanish video clips (short movies, TV series, and programmes) whose topics were related to the students' academic course content, over 12 weeks. Data gathered through podcasts, three questionnaires, and the teacher-researcher's notes was quantitatively and qualitatively analysed. Six podcasts produced by each participant (three recorded before dubbing and three after) were examined. The number of words spoken per minute in the first minute of the recording were calculated for each podcast after manual transcriptions. The podcasts recorded after the dubbing task show that students had increased their speed by an average of 17 words per minute. Podcasts were assessed by four external evaluators with regard to a number of oral expression criteria: speed, intonation, pronunciation, easy to follow speech, vocabulary, and grammar. On average, the evaluator found improvements in all the criteria. Podcast analysis also allowed to identify the sounds pronounced incorrectly by the students. In general, participants found consonants harder to pronounce than vowels. Students' answers to the three questionnaires show that after dubbing they perceived an increase in their confidence and ability to pronounce specific sounds. They believed they had improved in speed, intonation, and pronunciation in this order. In addition, they felt they had developed all four traditional skills, speaking in particular. Learning was also observed in vocabulary acquisition, and, to a lesser extent, in grammar knowledge. The dubbing task was also positively valued for its motivational factor. The teacher-observers confirmed the students' perceptions and provided useful feedback on how to improve dubbing tasks (vocabulary search, video selection, and session length). The teacher-researcher's notes report weekly impressions on class dynamics, video clips, and technical equipment. Overall, findings show concurrent improvement in pronunciation, intonation, and speed, thus corroborating the pilot's results (Sánchez Requena, 2016).

Talaván and Costal (2017) undertake an intralingual dubbing project (iDub) to assess its potential on the development of speaking skills. iDub is based on iCap, a previous project on intralingual captioning for the enhancement of writing skills and vocabulary acquisition (Talaván et al., 2016b). In view of its positive outcome, the ten ClipFlair activities (based on excerpts of an American sitcom and specifically created for the iCap project) were used in iDub, changing the task from subtitling to dubbing. The study involved 25 B2-level undergraduate students of English at UNED, Spain, in distance learning over two months. However, as often happens in online learning settings, only ten students completed all the activities and all data collection tools. Besides collecting data for research purposes, the study offers general guidelines for dubbing-task assessment. Assessment was carried out using an *ad hoc* rubric. In order to evaluate students' oral production and obtain quantifying dubbing task results for research purposes, the rubric includes the following assessment criteria.

- Accuracy: The voice recordings are grammatically correct.

- Synchrony: There is synchrony between the duration of each voice recording and the duration of the original actor's corresponding utterances.

- Pronunciation: The voice recordings are pronounced correctly.

- Intonation: Intonation is natural.

- Performance/dramatisation of the dialogues: Performance resembles the original utterance. (Talaván & Costal, 2017, p. 76)

The data was gathered through three tools: language assessment tests, questionnaires, and observation. The pre- and post-language assessment tests aimed at testing the level of oral proficiency in terms of pronunciation and fluency. The pronunciation test required participants to record a script taken from a humorous video; the fluency test required them to record a two to three-minute spontaneous speech excerpt. The average marks of the four tests – assessed by two observers – show a slight improvement in pronunciation and a greater enhancement of fluency after the dubbing task. Questionnaires indicate that students' perception of their L2 improvement is significant, especially in terms of speaking and listening, and to a lesser degree in terms of reading and writing. These last skills were also fostered during the project in preparing the dubbing script and while communicating with peers in the virtual learning environment. The great majority of participants reported that they would like to dub again and all of them would opt to dub a TV series. On the whole, learners found intralingual dubbing a motivating, albeit demanding, task. These perceptions were confirmed by means of observation during the entire project: forum exchanges, dubbing assessment tasks, and the final videoconference.

In the forums, students provided valuable peer-to-peer feedback on the final dubbed products:

> "[Student]2: [Student]1 as usual has an awesome accent, she sounds like a native, on the other hand some of the dubs are cut at the end. [Student]4 is so natural. Besides, your dub is probably one of the most accurate relating to the time. And finally, [Student]3, it is breathtaking the way you improve your dub from the first one to the last task, even with quick chunks that are very difficult to achieve" (Talaván et al., 2016b, p. 79).

The videoconference also produced useful feedback in view of a possible replication of the study. Many participants pointed out that dubbing ten videos, although short, over two months was too demanding in terms of time. The authors acknowledge that dubbing each two-minute long video required students two to three hours on average plus the time dedicated to forum interventions. The average scores of the dubbing tasks assessed with the *ad hoc* rubric were satisfying (6.7 out of 10), especially for intonation (1.9 out of 2) and pronunciation (1.6 out of 2). This can be interpreted in terms of learners' keenness to imitate as suggested in the task instructions, attempting to sound as natural as possible. Due to the small sample, findings cannot be generalised but offer a good starting point for future research.

3.2.   Audio description

Audio description is a narrative technique which translates the visuals into words, providing complementary information regarding the where, who, what and how of a given audiovisual excerpt during silent intervals. Its main purpose is to make an audiovisual product accessible to everybody (Maszerowska,

Matamala, & Orero, 2014). In the last two decades, there has been an increasing interest in AD in Translation Studies (Díaz Cintas, Orero, & Remael, 2007; Jiménez Hurtado, 2007; Matamala & Orero, 2016; Perego, 2012; among others). Scholars have also identified the potential of AD in foreign language learning and carried out a considerable amount of research in a limited period of time[5]. Learners can perform the intersemiotic process by creating an AD script in which they describe the visual of an AV product when it is not accompanied by dialogue, and record their voices. In general, the audiodescriptor "describes the scenery (place and time), the physical attributes (age, ethnic group, appearance, outfit, facial expressions, body language…), and sometimes the emotional state of characters, as well as their actions (perception and movements) […] with a ratio of 180 words per minute" (Ibáñez Moreno & Vermeulen, 2013, p. 43). Following the recommendations of professional practice, descriptions should be as objective and accurate as possible (Perego, 2014). Learners should be aware that they should not give more information than that which is perceived by a non-visually impaired spectator. As with dubbing and subtitling, learners should identify the most relevant information and respect time constraints[6]. The golden rule, then, is to find the right balance between describing too much and too little (Perego, 2014).

Within the ClipFlair project, Gajek and Szarkowska (2013) describe their AD and subtitling experience with undergraduate students and future-language teachers of Polish at the University of Warsaw, Poland. Students were introduced to ClipFlair and prepared a number of AD and subtitling activities for all levels of proficiency (A1-C2). To this purpose, teachers-to-be were required to respect copyright compliance in video selection and informed themselves about Creative Commons licences. ClipFlair activities were tested in the classroom and some problems with AV material were observed. For instance, poor image or sound

---

5. Like dubbing and subtitling, AD has been employed in translator training for enhancing writing (Clouet, 2005) and translation skills (Cambeiro Andrade & Quereda Herrera, 2007). Furthermore, in order to promote accessibility, Guedes (2010) (as cited in Rodrigues Barbosa, 2013, p. 490) advocates for the integration of AD in its broader sense in daily teaching and learning routines. A number of studies have focussed on the benefits of AD as a pedagogical tool for promoting learning and enhancing social inclusion in the classroom with and without visually-impaired people (Fiorucci, 2017; Walczak & Szarkowska, 2012). However, these considerations go beyond the scope of this work.

6. In order to respect time constraints, an interesting practical suggestion possible to apply in language learning is to anticipate relevant information that otherwise could be lost (Perego, 2014).

quality and excessively long videos decreased interest in the content of the video. This small-scale study shows that AVT-activity creation was a valuable and motivating exercise for future teachers. The study thus makes clear the need for a systematic development of language teaching methodologies with the use of subtitles and AD, as well as a more comprehensive search for examples of good practice.

Rodrigues Barbosa (2013) suggests AD as a language learning tool for teaching Spanish as a foreign language, describing an AD project. Following the main steps for the preparation of an AD (Benecke, 2004) and adapting them for pedagogical purposes, Rodrigues Barbosa (2013) made students listen to the soundtrack of a scene from a Spanish movie without showing them the video and asked them to advance hypotheses on the plot in L2. Students were surprised to see that their hypotheses did not coincide with the actual movie images. This preparatory exercise helped them understand the importance of the images for the correct understanding of an AV product, and the value of AD for visually-impaired people. They then prepared an individual draft of their AD script and tried to synchronise it with the video using Windows Movie Maker. During the voice recording, the scripts were changed to fit time constraints and particular attention was paid to pronunciation. In addition, grammar mistakes were corrected in the final version. According to the author, the AD task benefited writing and speaking skills as well as grammar knowledge.

Burger (2016) proposes AD as a novel task in teaching German as a foreign language, and provides detailed guidelines on how to carry out AD tasks with B1-B2 learners. It is recommendable to use very short scenes for the selected video, which contain brief dialogues and music and, ideally, a clearly recognisable sequence of events. As a preparatory exercise to make students aware of the importance of the images, the author suggests asking learners to keep their eyes closed or to sit so that they cannot see the screen. The learners are encouraged to check whether their description and vocabulary choices were accurate enough. A trial voice-recording session is advisable, since often the scripts are too long and must be reduced to be properly synchronised to the video. This trial revoicing can also serve to correct language mistakes.

Herrero and Escobar (2018) advocate for the integration of AD and Film Literacy Education in the foreign language curriculum. Starting from the idea that film and AD are powerful language learning tools, the authors believe that learners should be trained on how to effectively perform AD, and how they can develop active viewing strategies. In the context of teaching Spanish as a foreign language in higher education, the authors propose a pedagogical model designed to assist learners in developing linguistic and (inter)cultural competences while fostering critical appreciation of films. Using AD in language learning enables learners to acquire a range of language and transferable skills, in particular creativity and critical thinking. The principles of the pedagogical model are described as follows.

- The importance of merging language and content in the curriculum.

- The understanding that a wider range of multimodal texts should be part of the language curriculum.

- Films are multimodal texts and, therefore, they transmit information through a combination of semiotic systems [...].

- Audiovisual text and films in particular are ideal tools for raising students' cultural and intercultural awareness as they allow for reflection on discourse practices as situated discourses (historically and culturally).

- Film Literacy is an essential competence that language teachers and students should master.

- AD is a multiliteracy-oriented task that integrates both analytical and creative components (awareness, analysis, reflection and creative language use).

- AD projects enhance language learners' linguistic, cultural, and intercultural competences. They comprise encoding and decoding as fundamental processes for AD tasks (Herrero & Escobar, 2018, pp. 38-39).

The model aims at developing the following main competences: skills and knowledge related to language; technology, interaction, production, and dissemination processes; ideology and value; and aesthetics. The model is built on two case studies carried out in the UK. One took place with B2-level undergraduate students of Spanish, and the other with secondary-school learners of Spanish. The model envisages three sessions. In the first session, learners are introduced to film language and encouraged to develop their critical understanding of movies. The second session centres on the Spanish director Pedro Almodovar, and his movie *Broken Embraces*. The movie is based on the story of a visually impaired filmmaker, thus giving the chance to introduce AD as an accessibility mode, similar to AV products used in other studies presenting visually-impaired characters (Ibáñez Moreno & Vermeulen, 2013, 2014). Finally, the third session focusses on actual performance of the AD task. Preliminary findings indicate a considerable improvement in film literacy and accessibility awareness.

Experimental studies on the potential benefits of AD in foreign language learning conducted in the last decade are outlined in Table 3.3.

Table 3.3. Experimental studies on AD in chronological order

Author(s) and date of publication	Research focus	Target language (into L2)	Participants	Learning setting	Audiovisual material	AD software	Type of analysis
Ibáñez Moreno & Vermeulen, 2013	Lexical and phraseological competence	Spanish	52 B2-level undergraduate students in Belgium	Face-to-face	Movie	N/A	Qualitative and quantitative
Ibáñez Moreno & Vermeulen, 2014	Integrated learning skills	Spanish	13 Spanish-speaking university Erasmus and 12 Dutch-speaking university students in Belgium	Face-to-face	Movie	N/A	Qualitative

Ibáñez Moreno & Vermeulen, 2015a	Speaking skills (VISP)	English	16 B1-level Erasmus university students in Belgium	Face-to-face	Movie	VISP mobile app	Qualitative
Ibáñez Moreno & Vermeulen, 2015b	Speaking skills (VISP)	English	Ten B1-level Spanish undergraduate Erasmus students and ten Belgian undergraduate students in Belgium.	Online	Movie	VISP mobile app	Qualitative and quantitative
Ibáñez Moreno & Vermeulen, 2015c	Speaking skills (VISP)	English	12 Spanish (2 undergraduates in Spain, ten Erasmus students in Belgium) and ten undergraduate students in Belgium. All B1 level	Online	Movie	VISP mobile app	Qualitative
Cenni & Izzo, 2016	AD potential	Italian	20 B2-level undergraduate students in Belgium	Face-to-face	Movie	N/A	Qualitative
Talaván & Lertola, 2016	Speaking skills	English	30 B1-level English for specific purposes university students in Spain	Online	Tourist advertisement	ClipFlair	Qualitative and quantitative
Navarrete, 2018	Speaking skills	Spanish	6 university students in England	Face-to-face	Documentary	ClipFlair	Qualitative and quantitative
Calduch & Talaván, 2018	Writing skills	Spanish	15 B1-B2 level university students in England	Face-to-face	Movie	ClipFlair	Qualitative and quantitative

Ibáñez Moreno and Vermeulen (2013) explore AD as a tool for improving lexical and phraseological competence in the foreign language classroom within the Ghent University-based project *Audiodescripción como Recurso Didáctico en ELE* (ARDELE – Audio Description as a Didactic Resource for Spanish as a Foreign Language). The project involved 52 Dutch-speaking Belgian undergraduate B2-level Spanish students. The students were divided into three groups of 14, 29, and 9 participants respectively for practical reasons. Three four-minute clips were taken from a Spanish movie which tells the story of a woman who becomes blind after an accident. The movie was selected because its content could help sensitise students about visual-impaired conditions, and because it only contains a small amount of dialogue, thus maximising time for AD.

Each group had to audio describe one of the three video clips. The main goal of the study was to investigate whether the narrative content of the AV product influences learners' development of lexical and phraseological competence as well as to assess their motivation. To do this, data was gathered through controlled observation, two assignments (a first version of the AD task and, after correction and discussion, a second version of the task), and a final questionnaire. The AD task was organised into three phases: preparation, production, and review/final reflection. The first phase introduced students to AD by providing a set of basic rules (Ibáñez Moreno & Vermeulen, 2013, p. 48).

- Use only present tenses.

- Describe only sounds that visually impaired people cannot [perceive].

- Do not use expressions such as "we see…".

- Describe what you see, not what you think you see.

- Be concise.

The authors point out that the AD rule of using present tenses could limit AD as a pedagogical tool in foreign language learning but do not exclude possible variations. The AD-script-production phase required students to write the script individually, then review a classmate's script, carry out a group discussion, and finally select the most adequate script collaboratively. In the four-hour final phase, learners analysed their linguistic errors based on peer-to-peer and teacher's feedback. After the analysis, they repeated the AD task, which consisted in preparing the L2 scripts, and consequent metalinguistic reflection, but did not involve actual revoicing of the AD text. In light of the results – from observations, tasks, and questionnaires – the authors determine that AV selection influences the development of lexical competence, and that AD in particular contributes to the development of lexical and phraseological competence. Finally, the authors argue that the social value of AD makes it a very motivating activity for language learners.

In a different study, Ibáñez Moreno and Vermeulen (2014) investigate how AD can enhance integrated language skills – reading, writing, listening, and speaking – and intercultural competence through a case study carried out at the University College at Ghent, Belgium. The case study involved two groups of students: Group A, which comprised 13 Spanish-speaking Erasmus students (attending an English-Spanish AVT course), and group B, which included 12 Dutch-speaking students of Spanish (attending a Dutch-Spanish AVT course). The AV material selected was *Blind* by Tamar van den Dop, the first Dutch movie with AD. The movie is inspired on Hans Christian Andersen's fairy tale *The Snow Queen*, and tells the story of a young blind man. As in other studies (Herrero & Escobar, 2018; Ibáñez Moreno & Vermeulen, 2013), the content served to familiarise learners to the issue of accessibility.

Both groups were introduced to the movie and basic AD rules. Group A performed intersemiotic translation in L1 by describing one silent three-to-five-minute excerpt of the movie (with a ratio of 180 words per minute, resulting in a range of 540-900 words) with the teacher's supervision in two hours. Students' AD scripts were compared with the original AD script translated by the teacher from Dutch into Spanish. Comparison of the two versions shows that learners' scripts are less concise. Discussion of the two versions gave rise to a number of reflections on how learners can improve their AD. After the common general introduction to the task, Group B performed an oral comprehension exercise on a few fragments of the AD (with no images) made by Group A to identify the most relevant characteristics of an AD script and thus promote language awareness. Then, Group B students compared Group A's AD scripts with the original AD script translated by the teacher to foster metalinguistic reflection. Afterwards, Group B participants audio described other fragments of the movie in Spanish. Working in pairs, one of the students orally described the images to the other, who was taking notes on what was said, and not looking at the screen. In this way, the student taking notes could check whether the description was sufficiently clear to understand what was going on in the movie. The roles were then inverted to allow all students to practice speaking skills on one hand, and listening and writing skills on the other. Finally, the AD versions of both groups were compared in terms of language and image perception in order to enhance intercultural competence. Overall, Group A dedicated eight hours to the project, and Group B ten hours.

Ibáñez Moreno and Vermeulen (2013) claim that the intersemiotic task in L1 and L2 provided useful material for carrying out contrastive analysis both in linguistic and intercultural terms. In particular, the AD task allowed learners of Spanish as a foreign language to foster their integrated language skills in a motivating way. However, they mentioned three limitations in the application of AD tasks in language learning. Two of these are more general, and have already been stated above: the AD rule of using present tense, and the limited amount of time for the description (Ibáñez Moreno & Vermeulen, 2013). The third is more specifically related to Spanish as an L2 since in AD the grammatical subject is specified much more often than is done in common language use.

Ibáñez Moreno and Vermeulen (2015a) continued their research on the use of AD in the foreign language classroom by developing VIdeos for SPeaking (VISP), a mobile app based on AD to promote English language learning for Spanish students. The researchers present a case study testing the pilot mobile assisted language learning app version carried out with 16 Spanish Erasmus students of English as a foreign language (level B1) at the Ghent University, Belgium. The case study aimed at exploring the use of AD in an app for the promotion of oral speaking skills, vocabulary learning, and intercultural competence. The pilot app version required learners to

> "1) read a small introduction to AD, watch an example and complete a pre-test questionnaire, 2) view a clip, 3) draft a small AD script (if necessary) for the clip, 4) record the AD script over the clip (that is, produce an audio described clip), and 5) complete a final questionnaire" (Ibáñez Moreno & Vermeulen, 2015a, p. 133).

The post-questionnaire required learners to self-evaluate their AD of the 30-second clip taken from the movie *Moulin Rouge* by Baz Luhrmann, by comparing it with the official DVD's AD. In particular, participants evaluated how they described the video's time and setting, and the characters' aspects and moods. Results from the questionnaire and AD scripts show that participants overestimated their performance. Although proving to be a motivating task, the amount of vocabulary learned was limited and the researchers planned to improve the app.

Ibáñez Moreno and Vermeulen (2015b) assess the validity of the finalised mobile assisted language learning app VISP in promoting oral production by testing it with two groups of users. One group was comprised of ten Spanish Erasmus and the other group of ten undergraduate Belgian students of English as a foreign language (level B1) at the Ghent University, Belgium. The app is designed for B1 learners of English and offers learners the opportunity to carry out an AD task on a 30-second clip. The average AD session lasts 30 minutes and can be paused and resumed with no restrictions. Although in the professional AD practice 180 words per minute are recommended for descriptions, the VISP app – specifically designed for language learning – allows for a maximum of 60 words per minute. Following the basic principles of mobile learning, the app provides essential information on AD and a real AD sample to instruct users on how to perform the task. Apart from giving personal data in order to receive feedback on the task, learners can take a ten-question language test that contains vocabulary useful for carrying out the AD task. The app allows learners to watch the video as many times as they wish, to record their AD, to listen to their own performance and, finally, to submit their version. If they provide their personal data, they will receive feedback, otherwise the AD recording will be stored by the app managers in order to keep track of the users' tasks. In addition, users can also fill in a self-evaluation questionnaire (Ibáñez Moreno & Vermeulen, 2015a).

The app was sent by email to participants, who downloaded it and used it. The instruments used to compile data in this study were those integrated in the app; namely, the pre- and post-questionnaires, as well as the students' AD recordings. The case study results show that VISP better motivated Spanish students. However, Belgian students demonstrated better language performance, generally providing more accurate as well as grammatically and lexically correct descriptions. The authors came to the conclusion that mobile assisted language learning apps should take into account learners' native language and culture. Furthermore, they suggest that these types of apps should be used in blended learning or classroom settings as a resourceful tool to support teaching rather than being the ultimate focus.

Ibáñez Moreno and Vermeulen (2015c) present a new version of the mobile assisted language learning app, VISP 2.0, resulting from improvements based on feedback received on its previous versions. The new VISP app was tested by 12 Spanish students (2 undergraduates at UNED, Spain, and ten Erasmus students at Ghent University, Belgium) and ten Belgian students of English at Ghent University, Belgium. Students' responses to pre- and post-questionnaires and their AD tasks confirm previous findings (Ibáñez Moreno & Vermeulen, 2015a, 2015b). The ten Belgian students and the two UNED students' performances were more accurate compared to those of the Spanish Erasmus students. However, the Spanish Erasmus students showed a better attitude towards their performance and the app. As future app improvements, the authors envisage giving alternative options to users who do not wish to complete the questionnaires[7].

---

7. Ibáñez Moreno, Jordano, and Vermeulen (2016a) and Ibáñez Moreno, Vermeulen, and Jordano (2016b) report on the creation and launch of VISP and the process that led to the creation of the second version VISP 2.0, which is described in great detail.

Cenni and Izzo (2016) present the results of an exploratory study aimed at evaluating the potential of AD in teaching Italian as a foreign language at Ghent University, Belgium. The study involved 20 B2-level undergraduate students of Italian over three two-hour sessions. Students were instructed to audio describe two excerpts of an Italian movie. The movie was selected because it was a comedy presenting typical Italian stereotypes, and because the authors had the official AD transcript. The two four-minute excerpts presented limited dialogues and a dynamic series of events, so that the students had a number of characters and situations to describe. In the first session, after explaining basic AD rules to be followed (i.e. do not interrupt dialogues, offer precise objective descriptions in the present tense, etc.), learners were divided into small groups. Half of the groups wrote the AD script of the first excerpt and the other half the script of the second; all AD scripts were corrected by the teachers. The most frequent mistakes made by students are described in great detail, and are related to morpho-syntactic, lexical, and cultural aspects. The authors believe that part of the errors were due to the nature of AD, which requires an accurate description, in other words, being lexically precise and concise. In the second session, peer-to-peer feedback was carried out: each group corrected the AD script of the excerpts written by another group so that all students had the chance to see both excerpts. Then all groups received the teachers' corrections and, finally, the official AD script. Students were encouraged to conduct a metalinguistic analysis by comparing the three AD versions. In the last session, students took a translation test where they had to translate a number of sentences and words from L1 (Dutch) into L2 (Italian). The translation test results were satisfactory since they show that metalinguistic reflections helped students to improve their knowledge of new structures. Similarly to AD activities carried out by Ibáñez Moreno and Vermeulen (2013) and González Davies (2004), this activity included no actual revoicing. This is because the task focussed on writing the AD-script in L2 and comparing it with peers' versions as well as the official AD transcript. Overall, the paper shows that AD could be an effective language learning tool since it encourages metalinguistic reflection, thus promoting language and intercultural awareness.

Talaván and Lertola (2016) investigate the potential of AD in enhancing speaking skills in foreign language distance-learning using ClipFlair. The quasi-experimental study was carried out with 30 B1-level English for specific purposes (Tourism) undergraduate students at UNED, Spain, over two months. Participants were equally divided into two groups: experimental and control. Experimental group participants were further divided into three four-member and one three-member subgroups. They were asked to collaboratively write the AD script of two tourist advertisements, then record their scripts individually using ClipFlair. Two weeks of time was given for the AD of each video. Control group participants continued with their regular course activities. Data gathering instruments included language assessment tests, initial and final questionnaires, and observations made by two observers throughout the entire project (via forums, chats, assessments, and a final video conference). An oral pre-test was administered one week before starting the project, and an oral post-test at the end. The two oral-language tests were taken by the learners online using videoconference software on UNED's virtual learning environment. After listening to a number of questions related to tourism, learners had five minutes to prepare their monologue on the required topics. Finally, they had to record themselves discussing such topics for three to five minutes. The oral pre- and post- tests were assessed by two observers following an assessment rubric comprising four 2.5-point-scale criteria (pronunciation/ intonation, fluency, vocabulary, and grammar). Analysis of average marks shows a significant difference between experimental group scores in the oral pre- and post-tests, thus indicating that the AD tasks enhanced the experimental group's speaking skills. However, no differences were found between the two groups in terms of statistical analysis. According to final questionnaire responses, AD met the expectations of all the students involved with respect to language skills improvement. Learners perceived a greater improvement in this order: oral production (revoicing); writing production (AD script writing, forum posts, and chat communication); oral comprehension (listening to their classmates' revoicing); and reading comprehension (forum posts, chat communication, and AD common script). Learners also recognised an improvement in their knowledge of grammar and vocabulary, as well as in their confidence of their English proficiency. The cooperative learning aspect was positively assessed by most of the learners, who found working together towards a common goal highly motivating. AD using ClipFlair was also positively evaluated by most participants who were eager to repeat the AD experience with similar videos or movies and practise other revoicing tasks. Direct observation of the final video conference complements previous findings since learners provided useful feedback. After some comments on the videos selected, learners identified text condensation as the most challenging aspect of the AD task. They showed great enthusiasm towards the project, and reiterated that it gave them a valuable opportunity to practise English.

Navarrete (2018) explores the potential of AD in the development of oral skills through a small-scale experimental study. The study involved six B1-level final-year undergraduate students of Spanish as a foreign language at Imperial College, London (12 students initially participated in the course but only half completed it). The author suggests that the reason for this high drop-out rate could be related to the fact that some of the students received no credits for the course or because they had not realised how demanding their final year could result. Data was collected through an oral pre-test, an AD task evaluation, and two questionnaires. Students were pre-tested by recording a podcast about themselves. Then, after being introduced to the topic of the video selected for the AD task, they actually carried out the AD task in ClipFlair. AD tasks were sent to the teacher for correction and, finally, students' samples were shown in the classroom to encourage peer-to-peer discussion regarding oral-performance aspects. The AD tasks were assessed following the same rubric used for the evaluation of the oral pre-test. The oral assessment rubric includes four criteria: pronunciation and intonation, fluency, vocabulary, and grammar. In order to evaluate the improvement of oral skills, the author examines the nature of fluency, pronunciation, and intonation in detail. Two questionnaires were also administered to collect students' perceptions of the two oral activities (podcast and AD). Navarrete (2018) acknowledges the limitations of the study; however, she considers that the positive responses of the learners to the AD task are encouraging and set the basis for further investigation.

Calduch and Talaván (2018) investigate whether AD can foster stylistic richness by enhancing vocabulary acquisition. The study presents the preliminary results of the employment of AD tasks in a course of Spanish as a foreign language at the University of Cambridge. The study involved 15 B1-B2 level students of Spanish who carried out the course over eight weeks for a total of 32 hours (16 hours in the classroom and 16 hours outside the classroom). The first session aimed at introducing AD to the participants as well as describing techniques. The other six sessions were devoted to AD practise through four AD tasks based on different two to three-minute video clips. After watching the video clip and brainstorming vocabulary, each AD task required students to write a draft of the AD text. Each task had a different writing sequence that focusses on individual, pair, or group work. The rationale was to examine which one was the most appropriate writing sequence. After writing the AD text, students could record their voices in ClipFlair. In the final session, students could evaluate and reflect on the learning experience.

For what concerned the data collection instruments, the study availed of a vocabulary pre-, post- and post-delayed test; AD texts; a final questionnaire after each task; a final group interview; and a course final questionnaire. The qualitative analysis presented in the article refers to five students who completed the required tasks. The course final questionnaire reported encouraging results since the students felt that they had improved their writing skills and this impression is confirmed by the comparison of their AD texts. In addition, the researchers notice an improvement in their lexical accuracy and syntax. The vocabulary post- and post-delayed test reveal that students better recalled words that they had used in the AD texts. In the final group interview and in the course final questionnaire, the students acknowledged that the AD tasks increased their motivation since they could try a new writing exercise based on enjoyable audiovisual material. Pair and individual work were the most appreciated by the participants. Although it was not the aim of the study, in the final group interview, the researchers observed an improvement in the participants' oral skills in terms of fluency and pronunciation which goes in line with previous studies (Ibáñez Moreno & Vermeulen, 2015a; Navarrete, 2018; Talaván & Lertola, 2016).

3.3. Voice-over

Voice-over is another revoicing technique, also known as 'half-dubbing', usually employed in documentaries and AV products that do not require lip synchronisation. It consists in an oral translation: a few seconds after the onset of the original spoken text, which is fully audible, the volume decreases and one can hear the recorded translation (Pérez González, 2009). Its use in the foreign language classroom is indeed very limited. The only experimental study on the application of voice-over in the foreign language classroom currently identified is presented in Table 3.4.

Table 3.4. Experimental studies on voice-over in chronological order

Author(s) and date of publication	Research focus	Target language (into L2)	Participants	Learning setting	Audiovisual material	AD software	Type of analysis
Talaván & Rodríguez-Arancón, forthcoming	Speaking skills	English	8 C1-level students in Spain	Online	Advertisement	N/A	Qualitative and quantitative

Talaván and Rodríguez-Arancón (forthcoming) carried out a project (VICTOR) aimed at assessing the potential of voice-over in the development of speaking skills, in particular pronunciation and intonation. The project involved eight C1 level Spanish students of English at UNED, Spain, who volunteered to participate. Over a period of two months, devoting three to four hours per week, students produced the revoiced versions of four video clips of short American advertisements from the 1950's and 60's, chosen among a list of ten, in an online environment. After watching video tutorials and a sample task, each students choose four video clips and started the revoicing tasks. First, they carried out a voice-over task, then, a guided-dubbing task, and finally, a creative revoicing. In the voice-over task, learners were required to transcribe the oral spoken text, and record the transcription starting a few seconds after the original, whose volume had been lowered. In the guided-dubbing task, learners had to create a new script (using a number of pre-selected words and expressions containing phonemes difficult to pronounce for Spanish speakers), and record their voices to substitute the original spoken text. In the creative revoicing task, learners were allowed to choose either dubbing or voice-over. Learners uploaded the three revoiced versions of the four video clips on a YouTube channel for self- and peer-to-peer evaluation.

Data was collected through oral language assessment, initial and final questionnaires, as well as observation. At the beginning of the project, learners had to complete the initial questionnaire (about general information on their proficiency and AV knowledge) and carry out a pre-test, which required learners to record a radio advertisement using a number of pre-selected words and expressions for about one minute. The final revoiced versions of the clips were analysed by comparing them with the pre-test. The analysis revealed oral production improvement, especially with regard to pronunciation of the selected challenging phonemes. For what concerned self- and peer-to-peer evaluation, it is interesting to notice that learners were particularly strict when assessing their own production by giving lower scores compared to those provided by their peers. In addition, self-evaluation of pronunciation and intonation is more similar to the evaluation provided by the researchers. However, synchrony was assessed similarly by peers and researchers with higher scores compared to those provided in the self-evaluation. The final questionnaire suggests that voice-over tasks could promote the development of integrated language skills, in particular oral comprehension. In general, the project met participants' expectations in terms of development of language and information and communications technology skills. In addition, learners claimed that the project had helped them to better know AVT, and resulted a very enjoyable activity for most of them. However, voice-over was the least preferred AVT mode in the project, researchers ascribe the possible reasons to the technical challenges and to the absence of the creative element. Almost all participants would like to repeat the experience which they considered innovative and positive for language learning.

Combined captioning and revoicing

The application of combined captioning and revoicing tasks in foreign language education has been gaining researchers' attention in the last few years. Specific attention has been paid to combined reverse interlingual captioning and revoicing in teaching and learning of English as a foreign language in the university context. To a smaller extent, combined intralingual captioning and revoicing has also been considered as an innovative teaching technique in higher education.

4.1. Combined reverse interlingual captioning and revoicing

A limited number of experimental studies on combined reverse interlingual subtitling and dubbing have been identified, as shown in Table 4.1. Reverse subtitling and dubbing tasks can foster language learning, particularly L2 written and oral production skills. In this context, AV material presents learners with a contextualised communicative situation in their L1 that they should convey in L2. Besides producing written and oral language in L2, the role of translation in this task can also enhance foreign language learning.

Talaván, Bárcena, and Villarroel (2014) investigate the potential of reverse subtitling combined with reverse dubbing in the process of competence transference through online collaboration in a higher education context. The authors carried out an experimental study with undergraduate students from two degree programmes – Tourism and English Studies (translation course) – at UNED, Spain. Students dubbed and subtitled a tourism video from Spanish into English. The video was carefully selected in order to suit the learners and the AVT tasks. It lasted six minutes and contained about 600 words, involving both narrative and dialogue, and an adequate amount of specialised terminology.

The experimental research project lasted ten weeks and involved 15 students (initially 21), who collaborated on the online platform of UNED. Students availed of Aegisub as a subtitling software and Audacity as a dubbing software. The tasks were done in four stages. First, learners were made familiar with the tasks and the software. Second, students from the translation course had to translate and subtitle the video with the supervision of tourism students for what concerned specialised vocabulary. Third, students of tourism had to dub the videos (i.e. translating and revoicing) with the assistance of translation students with regards to the translation task. Finally, all students were required to fill in a task-evaluation questionnaire. Collaborative work was mainly done through forums and, to a lesser extent, through chats. The qualitative results obtained from observations and the evaluation questionnaire are positive according to the research objectives. Results reveal that the students from the tourism degree paid particular attention to the linguistic and translation aspects of the task, thus improving their mediation competence, while the students of translation focussed on English for specific purposes language in order to properly subtitle and dub the tourism video from Spanish into English.

Talaván, Rodríguez-Arancón, and Martín-Monje (2015) study the enhancement of speaking skills through reverse dubbing and subtitling in distance-learning education. A total of 74 C1-level undergraduate students of English at UNED, Spain, were involved in this experimental research project over three months. The students were divided into two groups: experimental and control. The experimental group was comprised of 46 students, 26 of which were attending a translation course. These students were further divided into five six-to-eight person subgroups and asked to collaboratively perform dubbing and subtitling tasks on four two-minute-long clips extracted from the same Spanish movie. The experimental group participants had two weeks to dub and subtitle each clip. The software used for dubbing and subtitling was Windows Movie Maker and DivXLand Media Subtitler respectively. The control group included 28 students who continued their regular English language course. Seven teachers followed students' work and progress during the project. Quantitative and qualitative data was collected using a pre- and post-questionnaire, oral pre- and post-tests, task assessments, observations, and a final videoconference. As for the quantitative analysis, "[the] methods employed were correlation studies, average marks distribution and hypothesis testing [...] in order to provide the triangulation necessary to be able to obtain reliable results that could be generalised to a certain extent" (Talaván et al., 2015, p. 340).

Table 4.1. Experimental studies on combined reverse interlingual captioning and revoicing in chronological order

Author(s) and date of publication	Research focus	Target languages (from L1 to L2)	Participants	Learning setting	Audiovisual material	Captioning/ Revoicing software	Type of analysis
Talaván et al., 2014	Collaborative language learning	From Spanish into English	15 English for specific purposes university students in Spain	Online	Tourist advertisement	Captioning: Aegisub Revoicing: Audacity	Qualitative
Talaván et al., 2015	Speaking skills	From Spanish into English	74 C1-level undergraduate students in Spain	Online	Movie	Captioning: DivXLand Media Subtitler Revoicing: Windows Movie Maker	Qualitative and quantitative
Talaván & Ávila-Cabrera, 2015	Speaking and writing skills	From Spanish into English	56 C1-level undergraduate students Spain	Online	Movie	Captioning: DivXLand Media Subtitler Revoicing: Windows Movie Maker	Qualitative and quantitative
Lertola & Mariotti, 2017	Pragmatic awareness	From Italian into English	33 B1-level undergraduate students in Italy	Face-to-face	Advertisement	Captioning and Revoicing: ClipFlair	Qualitative and quantitative

The quantitative analysis showed that students' oral production had improved after performing dubbing and subtitling tasks. The qualitative analysis supported results obtained from quantitative data. Most of the students felt they had improved their oral skills (speaking and listening). In addition, collaborative work was seen as particularly valuable to promoting language learning.

Talaván and Ávila-Cabrera (2015) examine combined reverse dubbing and subtitling to develop oral and written production, as well as general translation skills in online education. A total of 56 C1-level undergraduate students of English at UNED, Spain, were involved in the quasi-experimental study. Participants were divided into two groups: 40 students formed the experimental group, and 16 students the control group. Further divided into five six-to-eight-person subgroups, experimental group participants collaboratively dubbed and subtitled four clips taken from a Spanish movie into English over eight weeks (two weeks for each clip). In order to carry out the AVT tasks, learners were urged to use various software programmes – Windows Movie Maker for dubbing, DivXLand Media Subtitler for subtitling, and Pocket DivX Encoder for adding the subtitles to the video. Similar to the phases defined by Talaván et al. (2015), the stages for performing collaborative dubbing and subtitling tasks online were as follows:

> "(1) the participants created a collaborative translation draft for the dubbing version (around 2 hour work, from day 1 to day 4); (2) they had two days (1 hour work approximately) to use that draft to individually dub the video using Windows Movie Maker and to share their versions in their subgroups so as to vote for their representative version; (3) then, the subtitling phase started with a similar structure, since first the students had two days (1 hour work approximately) to find a common draft of the translation adapted to the creation of subtitles (they were given specific guidelines in terms of condensation, omission strategies, etc.); (4) they spent another two days (around 1 hour work) individually subtitling the clip (with DivXLand Media Subtitler) using the common draft as a reference, to later share their final versions (merged by themselves with the help of Pocket DivX Encoder) and vote for a representative one within each subgroup" (Talaván & Ávila-Cabrera, 2015, p. 158).

Students' work and progress was supervised by four teachers and two tutors, who solved linguistic or technical issues and ensured that they followed the instructions given. At the end of the project, 40 representative versions (five dubbed and five subtitled per video and subgroup) were uploaded for evaluation. Quantitative and qualitative collection instruments included oral and written pre- and post-tests, initial and final questionnaires, direct and indirect observations, as well as a final videoconference. Positive results in both oral production and translation skills were highlighted by data analysis. Though learners devoted a greater amount of time to written production during the project, this improved to a lesser extent than oral production. The researchers ascribe the great enthusiasm participants acknowledged for the dubbing task to this difference. Interestingly, the final questionnaire shows that students perceived that they had improved more in their receptive skills (reading and listening) than in their productive skills (speaking and writing). In addition, a great majority of students recognised some improvement in vocabulary and grammar knowledge as well as in their use-of-English confidence. They also acknowledged a great advancement in their general translation skills. Ultimately, students were highly satisfied with the collaborative work, confirming findings from a previous study (Talaván et al., 2015).

Lertola and Mariotti (2017) explore the potential of combined reverse dubbing and subtitling on raising pragmatic awareness in B1-level English as a foreign language undergraduate students in an Italian university. One year before, a pilot study had been carried out in order to test the experimental design and the testing instruments, as well as ClipFlair's usability. Within a quasi-experimental study design, 33 students were divided into four groups: a seven-person group (Experimental RS) performed reverse subtitling tasks using ClipFlair; a second five-person group carried out reverse dubbing tasks (Experimental RD) using ClipFlair; a third eight-person group (Experimental T) did translation tasks (no subtitling or dubbing) on the same AV material used for reverse subtitling and dubbing tasks; and a fourth 13-person control group (Control) continued with regular English learning in which no traditional or AV translation was involved. The AV material selected consisted of three short commercials in Italian that the Experimental RS, Experimental RD, and Experimental T had to subtitle, dub or translate into English respectively in six weeks. The four groups conducted their activities in a classroom context. A pre-test was administered one week before learners had to perform the required tasks, and immediate and delayed post-tests were given one week and two weeks after completing the tasks respectively. Pre- and post-tests aimed at assessing pragmatic competence through a discourse completion task in the form of written role plays in which learners had to respond to the description of a discursive situation (complaint and request). As in previous studies on AVT in language learning, the limited number of participants did not allow for a generalisation about the results. However, in order to provide greater reliability, the study made use of triangulation by collecting quantitative and qualitative data. Data analysis showed that the four groups' pragmatic awareness improved over time, even though no statistically significant difference was determined between groups. Nevertheless, it should be noted that the Experimental RS group had the highest performance both in the post-immediate and post-delayed tests, followed by the Experimental RD. These findings indicate "that these activities have potential and should be further explored" (Lertola & Mariotti, 2017, p. 114). The feedback collected through a final questionnaire reinforce this impression. Learners' opinions towards reverse subtitling and dubbing was generally positive. Contrary to the findings of Talaván and Ávila-Cabrera (2015), the majority of Experimental RS participants found the captioning activity useful for language learning while only a few of the Experimental RD participants deemed the dubbing activity useful. This difference could be attributed to the technical issues with voice synchronisation in ClipFlair which all RD participants had encountered.

4.2. Combined intralingual captioning and revoicing

Experimental research on combined intralingual captioning and revoicing is particularly limited. The studies identified are presented in Table 4.2. Intralingual subtitling and revoicing involve a condensed transcription and a repetition of the original L2-spoken language in the case of the study conducted by López Cirugeda and Sánchez Ruiz (2013). Thus, these innovative combined tasks can benefit not only productive (writing and speaking) but also receptive (listening and reading) skills as the combination of AD and subtitles for the hard-of-hearing, as suggested by Herrero, Sánchez Requena, and Escobar (2017), implies the creation of AD scripts and hard-of-hearing subtitles. Although the study focusses on the development of a teaching model, by using these combined tasks learners could develop both writing and speaking skills.

Table 4.2. Experimental studies on combined intralingual captioning and revoicing

Author(s) and date of publication	Research focus	Target languages (from L2 into L2)	Participants	Learning setting	Audiovisual material	Captioning/ Revoicing software	Type of analysis
López Cirugeda & Sánchez Ruiz, 2013	Teacher training, oral and written production in L2	English	54 B1/B2-level undergraduate students in Spain	Face-to-face	*Ad hoc* (created by learners)	Captioning: AVI Subtitler, DivXLand Media Subtitler and Subtitle workshop Revoicing: Virtualdub	Qualitative
Herrero et al., 2017	Pedagogical model	Spanish	B1/B2-level students in England	Face-to-face	Movie trailer	Captioning and Revoicing: Movie Maker	Qualitative

López Cirugeda and Sánchez Ruiz (2013) report on an experience carried out with 54 second year undergraduate students (B1-B2 levels) in primary education in the Faculty of Education in Albacete of the *Universidad de Castilla-La Mancha*, Spain. The primary task-based activity was intralingual subtitling; however, participants also performed intralingual revoicing tasks. The project pursued four main objectives: (1) to provide learners with the opportunity to create their own teaching material suitable for target children; (2) to plan a script demonstrating appropriate oral and written production in L2 (English); (3) to learn how to subtitle a video and be able to integrate subtitled videos, audio recordings, and slide presentations in their language teaching practice; and (4) to provide individual self-assessment on cooperative work through a written report. In addition, a group report was also submitted in order to identify the major difficulties encountered during the project.

The project was developed in four stages: initial (group and topic assignment); research (legal education framework study, materials and bibliography research, and subtitling workshops); production (script planning and writing, and video design with audio recording and subtitling); and post-production (video editing, final language review, and final activity presentation). During the research stage, when subtitling workshops took place (AVI Subtitler, DivXLand Media Subtitler and Subtitle), the teachers-to-be had to adapt general subtitling norms to the target audience (8-year-old children). In the production stage, after creating the video, students had to add intralingual English subtitles to their recordings. Although the focus of the article is on subtitling, the project also involves L2 captioning based on a text produced by the learners. During the final classroom presentation, the teachers-to-be presented the activities they had developed for primary school children. These activities required children to perform activities with subtitles as a support, such as practising listening and reading skills by filling the gaps with vocabulary available on the blackboard. Overall, the future teachers prepared appropriate activities for Primary school children, they produced correct subtitles considering that they had no previous experience and that several issues had arisen due to computer illiteracy. No precise data was given in the article regarding the learners' development of their oral and written production in L2, although this was among one of the primary objectives of the study. Only a general observation is provided, mentioned among the study's weaknesses: "[p]oor language level and insufficient didactic background were also apparent in their activities and, therefore, in their recordings" (López Cirugeda & Sánchez Ruiz, 2013, p. 54).

Herrero et al. (2017) present a study conducted by the Films, Languages, And Media in Education (FLAME) research group of the Manchester Metropolitan University which aims at developing a pedagogical method combining three disciplines – film literacy, AD, and deaf and hard-of-hearing subtitles – applied to foreign language learning. According to the model, learners can acquire film knowledge as well as the skills for carrying out AD and subtitles for the deaf and hard-of-hearing tasks. The teaching model has been tested with a group of B1-B2 level students of Spanish as a foreign language at the Manchester Metropolitan University. Two workshops for a total of ten hours were offered to the students as extra-curricular activities. Each workshop required learners to work two and a half hours in the classroom and two and a half hours outside the classroom. The AV material selected for the testing are two movie trailers since they are easy to find and there is no need to modify the original video for its class use. The movie trailers had Spanish standard subtitles to help learners with the video comprehension. After being introduced to the AVT modes, learners worked on the film analysis, with particular emphasis on the vocabulary necessary for each AV material, and carried out the AVT tasks. Since both AD and subtitles for the deaf and hard-of-hearing are modes aimed at making AV products accessible to visually impaired people and deaf and hard-of-hearing respectively, learners were introduced to the two practices by experiencing the video trailers either blindfolded or without the sound. In order to carry out the AVT tasks (i.e. adding the voice and subtitles to the video), learners used Movie Maker. After the workshops, learners were assessed for the final film analysis, AD, and subtitles for the deaf and hard-of-hearing they had produced. The article includes one assessing rubric for the film analysis, and one for both AD and subtitles for the deaf and hard-of-hearing. The evaluating criteria for AD and subtitles for the deaf and hard-of-hearing are the following: synchrony, content, pronunciation, intonation (AD), and vocabulary.

Results from the questionnaire conducted before and after each workshop reveal that most of the learners had a basic knowledge about cinema and accessibility before the workshops, and they increased considerably after attending them. In addition, most of them are interested in widening their knowledge on both topics. Overall, they expressed a positive opinion regarding the workshops. Almost all learners considered the workshops clear at a theoretical level, and all of them considered them useful at a practical level. In addition, they acknowledged AD as useful practice for knowing (inter)cultural elements as well as for practising oral skills, especially fluency and pronunciation. As for subtitles for the deaf and hard-of-hearing, all the learners believe that it is an effective task for practising vocabulary. On a technical level, most of the learners found Movie Maker appropriate for carrying out the revoicing and captioning tasks. Finally, the questionnaire contained two open-ended questions to which students answered that they had never experienced AV accessibility before, and that they better understand AD and subtitles for the deaf and hard-of-hearing modes. These results support the decision of the researchers to introduce film analysis and accessibility into two different future workshops.

Discussion

This work has sought to systematically review research on the applications of captioning and revoicing in language learning carried out in the last 20 years in order to offer an overview of the state of the art and encourage further research. The review of research on the use of the most widely studied AVT mode in language learning, namely captioning, illustrates how a number of publications have focussed on standard and reverse interlingual subtitling. Scholars argue for the integration of AVT tasks within a communicative approach to language learning and teaching. Interlingual subtitling is seen as an innovative and motivating exercise that allows learners to notice the language and negotiate meaning, thus enhancing listening comprehension and vocabulary acquisition (Díaz Cintas, 1995, 1997, 2001; Talaván, 2006a). Apart from the benefits deriving from translation, standard subtitling can prove particularly beneficial for improving listening skills, while reverse subtitling can enhance writing skills. In both cases, peer-to-peer review is encouraged to develop metalinguistic reflections. In research considering a teacher's perspective, examples of methodology-based subtitling models are also suggested for language learning and intercultural education (Borghetti, 2011; Incalcaterra McLoughlin & Lertola, 2011), as well as an adaptation of professional subtitling norms and assessment criteria for pedagogical purposes (Lertola, 2015). Finally, interlingual subtitling can also enrich language for specific purposes education (Kantz, 2015; Talaván, 2006b).

The greatest number of experimental studies focus on standard interlingual subtitling as a pedagogical tool. The benefits of interlingual subtitling have been identified with regards to listening comprehension (Talaván, 2010, 2011; Talaván & Rodríguez-Arancón, 2014a), vocabulary acquisition (Lertola, 2012, forthcoming), idiomatic expression retention (Bravo, 2008), intercultural education (Borghetti & Lertola, 2014), and pragmatic awareness (Incalcaterra

McLoughlin, 2009a; Incalcaterra McLoughlin & Lertola, 2016; Lopriore & Ceruti, 2015). In all the studies considered, English is one of the two languages involved in the subtitling task. In almost half of cases identified and examined, English is the L2; Italian is the L2 in all the other studies found. The great majority of these studies have been carried out in face-to-face university contexts involving a minimum of ten participants whose language levels ranged from A1 to C1. The AV material generally used is a movie or sitcom excerpt to be subtitled with the software Learning via Subtitling, ClipFlair, or Subtitle Workshop. The type of analysis applied is both qualitative and quantitative. Concerning reverse interlingual subtitling, the research focus is the development of writing and translation skills (Burczyńska, 2015; Talaván et al., 2016a; Talaván & Rodríguez-Arancón, 2014b). In the three experimental studies available, a qualitative and quantitative analysis is carried out on reverse subtitling of movie excerpts (with Aegisub or Subtitle Workshop) with English as the L2. Two of the studies involve a great number of university students as participants in online learning settings (Talaván et al., 2016a; Talaván & Rodríguez-Arancón, 2014b), whereas investigation on the application of intralingual subtitling tasks in language learning is quite limited. To this regard, only two studies were identified, one of which combines the use of intralingual subtitling and dubbing. The study on intralingual subtitling alone reports encouraging results on writing skills enhancement in undergraduate distance learning students of English, who subtitled a sitcom excerpt using ClipFlair (Talaván et al., 2016b).

Revoicing as a language learning tool is gaining more scholarly attention. Within revoicing, dubbing has enjoyed the highest consideration as an AVT technique; however, audio description is starting to be viewed as another effective task in the foreign language classroom. The literature review shows that dubbing has been suggested by many authors among other communicative language activities, either with or without translation (Bilbrough, 2007; Duff, 1989; Kumai, 1996; Zohrevandi, 1994). For instance, González Davies (2004) makes a general dubbing task proposal, without specifying whether to use standard or reverse dubbing in which the core exercise is translation, since no actual revoicing is required. Two options in dubbing tasks not involving translation have been identified: 'simple video dubbing', which consists in substituting the original soundtrack with students' voices; and 'scenario creation', suitable for more advanced students who can prepare their own storyline and script for a muted video (Burston, 2005). While the first option mainly focusses on the improvement of listening and speaking skills, the second option can also enrich reading and writing skills and boost grammar and vocabulary knowledge. Dubbing thus provides similar pedagogical benefits to video making while saving classroom time and being less complex in terms of logistics. It still requires preparation for both teachers and learners, however, especially in technical terms. Peer-to-peer collaboration and public presentation of the dubbed product also prove to be strong motivators (Burston, 2005; Danan, 2010; Duff, 1989; Kumai, 1996).

Experimental research has mainly focussed on intralingual dubbing; only one experimental study on reverse interlingual dubbing was found. A limited number of experimental studies that combine reverse interlingual subtitling and dubbing were identified. As with experimental research on captioning, the target language in most intralingual-dubbing experimental studies is English, followed by Spanish. These studies focus on the enhancement of speaking skills, mainly in face-to-face secondary-school and university settings. The number of participants varies greatly and so do their proficiency levels. In most studies, qualitative and quantitative data are both gathered. Movie or TV series excerpts are the most preferred AV materials, and ClipFlair is the dubbing software selected both in face-to-face and distance learning (Navarrete, 2013; Talaván & Costal, 2017). The research focus of the qualitative study on reverse interlingual dubbing is the development of speaking and writing skills, since army students in the United States are required to dub a number of AV excerpts from English into Dari, Pashto, or Farsi (Danan, 2010).

Scholars have carried out a considerable amount of research on the application of AD in foreign language learning in the last decade. Again, as is the case for dubbing and subtitling, English is the target language in most AD experimental studies, followed by Spanish. In general, the focus of AD tasks is the development of speaking skills (Talaván & Lertola, 2016). However, lexical and phraseological competence, integrated learning skills, and writing skills have also been considered (Calduch & Talaván, 2018; Ibáñez Moreno & Vermeulen,

2013, 2014). Interestingly, a number of studies focus on the development of speaking skills in Chinese learners of English (Chiu, 2012; Florente, 2016; He & Wasuntarasophit, 2015). However, videos used in some of these studies exceed the recommended length of video clips in language education. In other studies with students of Spanish as a foreign language, the content of clips selected for AD tasks is related to blindness in order to introduce AD as an accessibility mode and sensitise learners on visually-impaired conditions (Herrero & Escobar, 2018; Ibáñez Moreno & Vermeulen, 2013, 2014). All the experimental studies on AD were carried out with university students (mainly in face-to-face contexts) whose language levels ranged from B1 to B2. Participants carried out the AD either with ClipFlair or the VISP mobile app. In half of the cases, only qualitative data was gathered.

The application of combined captioning and revoicing has also gained scholars' attention in the last few years. A limited number of experimental studies on combined reverse interlingual subtitling and dubbing have been identified. Although focussing on different aspects – speaking skills, pragmatic awareness, and collaborative language learning – all studies are carried out with a considerable number of university students of English, mainly in distance education settings (Talaván et al., 2014, 2015; Talaván & Ávila-Cabrera, 2015). Quantitative and qualitative collection techniques were used in almost all the studies. The captioning software selected was either Aegisub, DivXLand Media Subtitler, or ClipFlair; while the revoicing software consisted of Audacity, Windows Movie Maker, or ClipFlair. As previously mentioned, two studies on combined intralingual captioning and revoicing were identified. The first qualitative study by López Cirugeda and Sánchez Ruiz (2013) reports on an English subtitling and revoicing task within teacher training in a face-to-face university context. The AV material was created by each participant who performed the task using one subtitling software programme among those suggested (AVI Subtitler, DivXLand Media Subtitler, and Subtitle workshop) and Virtualdub as revoicing software. The second qualitative study by Herrero et al. (2017) combines film analysis, AD, and subtitles for the deaf and hard-of-hearing. Although the study aims at developing an *ad hoc* teaching model, these combined AVT tasks could foster writing and speaking skills.

All AVT tasks examined provide learners with the opportunity to benefit from authentic multimodal input and produce a tangible output, which helps develop a sense of communicative achievement. Teachers play an important role both in revoicing and captioning tasks. For instance, Danan (2010) reckons that, although more successful in terms of motivation, entirely student-led projects present more language-related mistakes. She suggests finding the right balance between teachers' control and learners' initiative through periodical guidance and feedback. Borghetti and Lertola (2014) also acknowledge that more opportunities for intercultural learning arise with teachers' input. The main limitations of employing AVT tasks in foreign language learning are the lack of ready-made activities, which is in part overcome by the advent of ClipFlair, and technology-related issues. The creation of tasks can be time consuming. In particular, selecting videos with suitable language and content for AVT tasks can prove challenging. Furthermore, learners should be computer-literate and have access to a computer (or a mobile in the case of AVT apps) with an internet connection. The employment of apps is still quite limited. Experimental studies often report technological issues related to the software used encountered by learners while performing captioning and revoicing tasks.

Overall, the literature review on captioning and revoicing in language learning has revealed that a fast-growing body of research supporting the integration of AVT tasks in the foreign language classroom, especially in English as a foreign language learning, is currently available. Nevertheless, the literature review provides suggestions for future research. Besides developing current lines of research, future investigation should bridge the current gaps according to several of the authors cited. In particular, it should foster research on reverse interlingual subtitling and dubbing, intralingual subtitling, and combined intralingual captioning and revoicing. Moreover, scholars urge future research involving different language combinations. Participants should also come from a variety of learning contexts other than higher education, and be in online or blended settings. Finally, although they provide encouraging outcomes, a very limited number of studies is currently available on the benefits of AVT tasks in language for specific purposes education and teacher training, calling for future research in these regards.

Conclusion

The last two decades have revealed a growing interest in the integration of AVT with a communicative approach to language learning and teaching. European institutions have acknowledged the benefits of AVT in the foreign language classroom by funding research-led projects like LeViS and ClipFlair, promoting language learning through interactive captioning and revoicing tasks. Captioning – interlingual and intralingual subtitling – provides learners with the opportunity to enhance their listening, reading, writing, and transferable skills. Revoicing – dubbing, audio description, and voice over tasks – can foster learners' speaking, reading, listening, and writing skills.

This work aimed at systematically reviewing studies carried out in the last twenty years on the applications of captioning and revoicing in the foreign language classroom so as to offer a state of the art and promote future research. The literature review has outlined the research carried out on the topic – especially in the teaching of English as a foreign language – focussing on relevant experimental studies that involve data collection and analysis. These empirical studies have been reviewed in terms of research focus, target languages, participants, learning settings, audiovisual materials, captioning/revoicing software, and type of analysis (i.e. qualitative and/or quantitative).

Scholars have mainly focussed their attention on the benefits of standard and reverse interlingual subtitling with regards to listening comprehension, vocabulary acquisition, integrated language skills, intercultural education, and pragmatic awareness. Investigation on intralingual subtitling in language learning is quite limited, and reports encouraging results in the development of writing skills. More recently, however, research has also shown the potential of dubbing and audio description tasks for improving oral language skills, concentrating on the development of fluency and intonation as well as vocabulary acquisition, writing and integrated language skills. Furthermore, the application of combined captioning and revoicing tasks has been gaining researchers' attention in the last few years. In particular, research has focussed on the use of combined reverse interlingual subtitling and dubbing, and combined intralingual captioning and revoicing for the development of speaking and writing skills as well as pragmatic awareness.

References

Ary, D., Cheser Jacobs, L., & Sorensen, C. K. (2009). *Introduction to research in education* (8th ed.). Wadsworth.

Baños, R., & Sokoli, S. (2015). Learning foreign languages with ClipFlair: using captioning and revoicing activities to increase students' motivation and engagement. In K. Borthwick, E. Corradini & A. Dickens (Eds), *10 years of the LLAS elearning symposium: case studies in good practice* (pp. 203-213). Research-publishing.net. https://doi.org/10.14705/rpnet.2015.000280

Barbe, K. (1996). Dubbing in the translation classroom. *Perspectives: Studies in Translatology, 4*(2), 255-274. https://doi.org/10.1080/0907676X.1996.9961291

Benecke, B. (2004). Audio-description. *META, 49*(1), 78-80. https://doi.org/10.7202/009022ar

Bilbrough, N. (2007). *Dialogue activities: exploring spoken interaction in the language class.* Cambridge University Press. https://doi.org/10.1017/CBO9780511733130

Bollettieri, R. M., Di Giovanni, E., & Rossato, L. (2014). New challenges in audiovisual translation. In R. M. Bollettieri Bosinelli, E. Di Giovanni & L. Rossato (Eds), *inTRAlinea Special Issue: Across Screens Across Boundaries.* http://www.intralinea.org/specials/article/new_challenges_in_audiovisual_translation

Borghetti, C. (2011). Intercultural learning through subtitling: the cultural studies approach. In L. Incalcaterra McLoughlin, M. Biscio & M. Á. Ní Mhainnín (Eds), *Audiovisual translation subtitles and subtitling. Theory and practice* (pp. 111-137). Peter Lang.

Borghetti, C., & Lertola, J. (2014). Interlingual subtitling for intercultural language education: a case study. *Language and Intercultural Communication, 14*(4), 423-440. https://doi.org/10.1080/14708477.2014.934380

Bravo, C. (2008). *Putting the reader in the picture: screen translation and foreign-language learning.* Doctoral Thesis. http://www.tesisenred.net/handle/10803/8771

Burczyńska, P. (2015). Reversed subtitles as a powerful didactic tool in SLA. In Y. Gambier, A. Caimi & C. Mariotti (Eds), *Subtitles and language learning* (pp. 221-244). Peter Lang.

Burger, G. (2016). Audiodeskriptionen anfertigen - ein neues Verfahren für die Arbeit mit Filmen. *Info DaF-Informationen Deutsch als Fremdsprache, 1*, 44-54.

Burston, J. (2005). Video dubbing projects in the foreign language curriculum. *CALICO Journal, 23*(1), 79-92. https://doi.org/10.1558/cj.v23i1.79-92

Byram, M. (2000). Assessing intercultural competence in language teaching. *Sprogforum 18*(6), 8-13.

Caimi, A. (2015). Introduction. In Y. Gambier, A. Caimi & C. Mariotti (Eds), *Subtitles and language learning* (pp. 9-18). Peter Lang.

Calduch, C., & Talaván, N. (2018). Traducción audiovisual y aprendizaje del español como L2: el uso de la audiodescripción. *Journal of Spanish Language Teaching, 4*(2), 168-180. https://doi.org/10.1080/23247797.2017.1407173

Cambeiro Andrade, E., & Quereda Herrera, M. (2007). La audiodescripción como herramienta didáctica para el aprendizaje del proceso de traducción. In C. Jiménez Hurtado (Ed.), *Traducción y accesibilidad. Subtitulación para sordos y audiodescripción para ciegos: nuevas modalidades de Traducción Audiovisual* (pp. 273-287). Peter Lang.

Casañ Núñez, J. C. (2017). Tareas de comprensión audiovisual con preguntas sobreimpresas en el vídeo: valoraciones de cinco profesores universitarios de español como lengua extranjera. *EuroAmerican Journal of Applied Linguistics and Languages, 4*(1), 20-39. https://doi.org/10.21283/2376905X.6.77

Cenni, I., & Izzo, G. (2016). Audiodescrizione nella classe di italiano L2. Un esperimento didattico. *Incontri, 31*(2), 45-60. https://doi.org/10.18352/incontri.10169

Chiaro, D. (2009). Issues in audiovisual translation. In J. Munday (Ed.), *The Routledge companion to translation studies* (pp. 141-165). Routledge.

Chiu, Y. (2012). Can film dubbing projects facilitate EFL learners' acquisition of English pronunciation? *British Journal of Educational Technology, 43*(1), E24-E27. https://doi.org/10.1111/j.1467-8535.2011.01252.x

Clouet, R. (2005). Estrategia y propuestas para promover y practicar la escritura creativa en una clase de inglés para traductores. *Actas del IX Simposio Internacional de la Sociedad Española de Didáctica de la Lengua y la Literatura*, 319-326.

Cohen, L., Manion, L., & Morrison, K. (2007). *Research methods in education*. Routledge. https://doi.org/10.4324/9780203029053

Colina, S., & Lafford, B. A. (2018). Translation in Spanish language teaching: the integration of a "fifth skill" in the second language curriculum. *Journal of Spanish Language Teaching, 4*(2), 110-123. https://doi.org/10.1080/23247797.2017.1407127

Council of Europe (2001). *Common European Framework for Languages: Learning, Teaching, Assessment*. Cambridge University Press.

Danan, M. (2010). Dubbing projects for the language learner: a framework for integrating audiovisual translation into task-based instruction. *Computer Assisted Language Learning, 23*(5), 441-456. https://doi.org/10.1080/09588221.2010.522528

Díaz Cintas, J. (1995). El subtitulado como técnica docente. *Vida Hispánica 12,* 10-14.

Díaz Cintas, J. (1997). Un ejemplo de explotación de los medios audiovisuales en la didáctica de lenguas extranjeras. In M. Cuéllar (Ed.), *Las nuevas tecnologías integradas en la programación didáctica de lenguas extranjeras* (pp. 181-191). Universitat de Valencia.

Díaz Cintas, J. (2001). *Teaching subtitling at university.* Paper presented at the Training Translators and Interpreters in the New Millennium, Portsmouth, University of Portsmouth. http://www.eric.ed.gov/PDFS/ED456647.pdf

Díaz Cintas, J., Orero, P., & Remael, A. (Eds). (2007). *Media for all. Subtitling for the deaf, audio description and sign language.* Rodopi.

Dörnyei, Z. (2007). Research methods in applied linguistics. Oxford University Press.

Duff, A. (1989). *Translation.* Oxford University Press.

Ferreira Gaspar, N. (2009). Translation as a fifth skill in EFL classes at secondary level. In A. Witte, T. Harden & A. Ramos de Oliveira Harden (Eds), *Translation in second language learning and teaching* (pp. 173-179). Peter Lang.

Fiorucci, A. (2017). Audio descrizione e didattica inclusiva. Una ricerca sulla comprensione da ascolto e la capacità di immedesimazione. *Form@re - Open Journal per la formazione in rete, 17*(2), 150-163. http://www.fupress.net/index.php/formare/article/view/20540/19320

Florente, I. L. (2016). *How movie dubbing can help native Chinese speakers' English pronunciation.* School of Education Student Capstones and Dissertations. http://digitalcommons.hamline.edu/hse_all/4099

Gajek, E., & Szarkowska, A. (2013). Audiodeskrypcja i napisy jako techniki uczenia się języka - projekt ClipFlair. Jezyki Obce w Szkole. *Unijna wieża Babel,* 106-110. http://jows.pl/content/audiodeskrypcja-i-napisy-jako-techniki-uczenia-się-języka---projekt-clipflair?page=3

Gambier, Y. (2003). Introduction: screen transadaptation. Perception and reception. In Y. Gambier (Ed.), *Special issue of The Translator, 9*(2), 171-189.

Gernsbacher, M.A. (2015). Video captions benefit everyone. *Policy Insights from the Behavioral and Brain Sciences, 2*(1), 195-202. https://doi.org/10.1177/2372732215602130

Ghia, E., & Pavesi, M. (2016). The language of dubbing and its comprehension by learner-viewers. A resource for second language acquisition? *Across Languages and Cultures, 17*(2), 231-252. https://doi.org/10.1556/084.2016.17.2.5

References

González Davies, M. (2004). *Multiple voices in the translation classroom: activities, tasks, and projects*. John Benjamins. https://doi.org/10.1075/btl.54

Guedes, L. C. (2010). Os usos pedagógicos da audiodescrição - uma tecnologia assistiva a serviço da inclusão social. *Revista Nacional de Tecnologia Assistiva, 3*, 10-16

Hadzilacos, T., Papadakis, S., & Sokoli, S. (2004). Learner's version of a professional environment: film subtitling as an ICTE tool for foreign language learning. In J. Nall & R. Robson (Eds), *Proceedings of World Conference on E-Learning in Corporate Government, Healthcare, and Higher Education* (pp. 680-685). AACE.

He, P., & Wasuntarasophit, S. (2015). The effects of video dubbing tasks on reinforcing oral proficiency for Chinese vocational college students. *Asian EFL Journal, 17*(2), 106-133.

Herrero, C., & Escobar, M. (2018). A pedagogical model for integrating film education and audio description in foreign language acquisition. In L. Incalcaterra McLoughlin, J. Lertola & N. Talaván (Eds), *Special issue of Translation and Translanguaging in Multilingual Contexts. Audiovisual translation in applied linguistics: beyond case studies, 4*(1), 31-55.

Herrero, C., Sánchez Requena, A., & Escobar, M. (2017). Una propuesta triple. Análisis fílmico, traducción audiovisual y enseñanza de lenguas extranjeras. *inTRAlinea Special Issue: building bridges between film studies and translation studies*. http://www.intralinea.org/specials/article/2245

Ibáñez Moreno, A., Jordano, M., & Vermeulen, A. (2016a). Diseño y evaluación de VISP, una aplicación móvil para la práctica de la competencia oral. *RIED. Revista Iberoamericana de Educación a Distancia, 19*(1), 63-81. http://www.redalyc.org/html/3314/331443195004/index.html

Ibáñez Moreno, A., & Vermeulen, A. (2013). Audio description as a tool to improve lexical and phraseological competence in foreign language learning. In D. Tsigari & G. Floros (Eds), *Translation in language teaching and assessment* (pp. 41-61). Cambridge Scholars Publishing.

Ibáñez Moreno, A., & Vermeulen, A. (2014). La audiodescripción como recurso didáctico en el aula de ELE para promover el desarrollo integrado de competencias. In R. Orozco (Ed.), *New directions on Hispanic linguistics* (pp. 263-292). Cambridge Scholars Publishing.

Ibáñez Moreno, A., & Vermeulen, A. (2015a). Using VISP (VIdeos for SPeaking), a mobile app based on audio description, to promote english language learning among Spanish students: a case study. *Procedia - Social and Behavioral Sciences, 178*, 132-138. https://doi.org/10.1016/j.sbspro.2015.03.169

Ibáñez Moreno, A., & Vermeulen, A. (2015b). Profiling a MALL app for english oral practice. a case study. *Journal of Universal Computer Science, 21*(10), 1339-1361. http://www.jucs.org/jucs_21_10/profiling_a_mall_app/jucs_21_10_1339_1361_moreno.pdf

Ibáñez Moreno, A., & Vermeulen, A. (2015c). VISP 2.0: methodological considerations for the design and implementation of an audio-description based app to improve oral skills. In F. Helm, L. Bradley, M. Guarda & S. Thouësny (Eds), *Critical CALL - proceedings of the 2015 EUROCALL conference, Padova, Italy* (pp. 249-253). Research-publishing.net. https://doi.org/10.14705/rpnet.2015.000341

Ibáñez Moreno, A., Vermeulen, A., & Jordano, M. (2016b). Using audio description to improve FLL students' oral competence in MALL: methodological preliminaries. In A. Pareja-Lora, C. Calle-Martínez & P. Rodríguez-Arancón (Eds), *New perspectives on teaching and working with languages in the digital era* (pp. 245-256). Research-publishing.net. https://doi.org/10.14705/rpnet.2016.tislid2014.438

Incalcaterra McLoughlin, L. (2009a). Inter-semiotic translation in foreign language acquisition: the case of subtitles. In A. Witte, T. Harden & A. Ramos de Oliveira Harden (Eds.), *Translation in second language learning and teaching* (pp. 227-244). Peter Lang.

Incalcaterra McLoughlin, L. (2009b). Subtitles in translators' training: a model of analysis. *Romance Studies, 27*(3), 174-185. https://doi.org/10.1179/174581509X455141

Incalcaterra McLoughlin, L., & Lertola, J. (2011). Learn through subtitling: subtitling as an aid to language learning. In L. Incalcaterra McLoughlin, M. Biscio & M. A. Ní Mhainnín (Eds), Audiovisual translation. Subtitles and subtitling (pp. 243-263). Peter Lang.

Incalcaterra McLoughlin, L., & Lertola, J. (2014). Audiovisual translation in second language acquisition: integrating subtitling in the foreign language curriculum. *Special issue of The Interpreter and Translator Trainer, 8*(1), 70-83. https://doi.org/10.1080/1750399X.2014.908558

Incalcaterra McLoughlin, L., & Lertola, J. (2015). Captioning and revoicing of clips in foreign language learning using ClipFlair for teaching italian in online learning environments. In C. Ramsey-Portolano (Ed.), *The future of Italian teaching. Media, new technologies and multi-disciplinary perspectives* (pp. 55-69). Cambridge Scholars Publishing.

Incalcaterra McLoughlin, L., & Lertola, J. (2016). Traduzione audiovisiva e consapevolezza pragmatica nella classe d'italiano avanzata. In M. La Grassa & D. Troncarelli (Eds), *Orientarsi in rete. Didattica delle lingue e tecnologie digitali* (pp. 244-264). Becarelli Edizioni.

References

Jiménez Hurtado, C. (Ed.) (2007). *Traducción y accesibilidad. Subtitulación para sordos y audiodescripción para ciegos: nuevas modalidades de Traducción Audiovisual.* Peter Lang.

Jüngst, H. E. (2013). The potential of integrating dubbing activities in the translation classroom. *Trans: Revista de Traductología, 17,* 103-114. https://doi.org/10.24310/TRANS.2013.v0i17.3230

Kantz, D. (2015). Multimodal subtitling - a medical perspective. In Y. Gambier, A. Caimi & C. Mariotti (Eds), *Subtitles and language learning* (pp. 269-292). Peter Lang.

Krashen, S. D. (1985). *The input hypothesis: issues and implications.* Longman.

Kumai, W. (1996). Karaoke movies: dubbing movies for pronunciation. *The Language Teacher Online, 20*(9). https://jalt-publications.org/tlt/departments/myshare/articles/2049-karaoke-movies-dubbing-movies-pronunciation

Laufer, B., & Hulstijn, J. (2001). Incidental vocabulary acquisition in a second language: the construct of task-induced involvement. *Applied Linguistics, 22*(1), 1-26. https://doi.org/10.1093/applin/22.1.1

Lertola, J. (2012). The effect of the subtitling task on vocabulary learning. In A. Pym & D. Orrego-Carmona (Eds), *Translation research project 4* (pp. 61-70). Universitat Rovira i Virgili. http://www.intercultural.urv.cat/media/upload/domain_317/arxius/TP4/5-Lertola.pdf

Lertola, J. (2015). Subtitling in language teaching: suggestions for language teachers. In G. Yves, A. Caimi & C. Mariotti (Eds), *Subtitles and language learning* (pp. 245-267). Peter Lang.

Lertola, J. (forthcoming). Second language vocabulary learning through subtitling. *Revista Española de Lingüística Aplicada.*

Lertola, J., & Mariotti, C. (2017). Reverse dubbing and subtitling: raising pragmatic awareness in Italian ESL learners. *JoSTrans-The Journal of Specialised Translation, 28,* 103-121. https://www.jostrans.org/issue28/art_lertola.pdf

López Cirugeda, I., & Sánchez Ruiz, R. (2013). Subtitling as a didactic tool. A teacher training experience. *Portalinguarum, 20,* 45-62. https://www.ugr.es/~portalin/articulos/PL_numero20/3%20%20Isabel%20Lopez.pdf

Lopriore, L., & Ceruti, M. A. (2015). Subtitling and language awareness: a way and ways. In Y. Gambier, A. Caimi & C. Mariotti (Eds), *Subtitles and language learning* (pp. 293-321). Peter Lang.

Ma, Q. (2009). *Second language vocabulary acquisition.* Peter Lang.

Maley, A., & Duff, A. (2005). *Drama techniques: a resource book of communication activities for language teachers* (3rd ed.). Cambridge University Press. https://doi.org/10.1017/CBO9780511733079

Martí Ferriol, J. L., & Martí Marco, M. R. (2016). El tráiler cinematográfico y la subtitulación en la didáctica de lenguas: aplicación práctica en la combinación lingüística alemán - español. *Revista de Lenguas para Fines específicos, 22*(2), 104-129.

Maszerowska, A., Matamala, A., & Orero, P. (Eds). (2014). *Audio description: new perspectives illustrated.* John Benjamins. https://doi.org/10.1075/btl.112

Matamala, A., & Orero, P. (Eds). (2016). *Researching audio description: new approaches.* Palgrave Macmillan. https://doi.org/10.1057/978-1-137-56917-2

Navarrete, M. (2013). El doblaje como herramienta de aprendizaje en el aula de español y desde el entorno Clipflair. *marcoELE, 16,* 75-87. http://marcoele.com/descargas/16/8.londres-2.pdf

Navarrete, M. (2018). The use of audio description in foreign language education: a preliminary approach. In L. Incalcaterra McLoughlin, J. Lertola & N. Talaván (Eds), *Special issue of Translation and Translanguaging in Multilingual Contexts. Audiovisual translation in applied linguistics: beyond case studies, 4*(1), 129-150.

Neves, J. (2004). Language awareness through training in subtitling. In P. Orero (Ed.), *Topics in audiovisual translation* (pp. 127-139). John Benjamins. https://doi.org/10.1075/btl.56.14nev

Orrego Carmona, D. (2013). Entrevista a Jorge Díaz Cintas: contexto actual de los estudios en traducción audiovisual. *Mutatis Mutandis, 6*(2), 549-560. https://www.researchgate.net/publication/314276847_Entrevista_a_Jorge_Diaz_Cintas_Contexto_actual_de_los_estudios_en_traduccion_audiovisual

Pavesi, M. (2012). The potentials of audiovisual dialogue for second language acquisition. In P. Alderete-Díez, L. Incalcaterra McLoughlin, L. Ní Dhonnchadha & D. Ní Uigín (Eds), *Translation, technology and autonomy in language teaching and learning* (pp. 155-174). Peter Lang.

Perego, E. (2005). *La traduzione audiovisiva.* Carocci.

Perego, E. (2012). *Emerging topics in translation: audio description.* EUT. https://www.openstarts.units.it/handle/10077/6356

Perego, E. (Ed.). (2014). *L'audiodescrizione filmica per i ciechi e gli ipovedenti.* EUT.

Perego, E. (2016). History, development, challenges and opportunities of empirical research in audiovisual translation. *Across Languages and Cultures, 17*(2), 155-162. https://doi.org/10.1556/084.2016.17.2.1

Pérez González, L. (2009). Audiovisual translation. In M. Baker & G. Saldanha (Eds), *Routledge encyclopedia of translation studies* (pp. 13-20). Routledge. https://doi.org/10.4324/9781315762975

Pérez-González, L. (2014). *Audiovisual translation: theories, methods and issues*. Routledge.

Ragni, V. (2018). Didactic subtitling in the foreign language (FL) classroom. Improving language skills through task-based practice and form-focused instruction (FFI): Background considerations. In L. Incalcaterra McLoughlin, J. Lertola & N. Talaván (Eds), *Special issue of Translation and Translanguaging in Multilingual Contexts. Audiovisual translation in applied linguistics: beyond case studies*, *4*(1), 10-30.

Robson, C. (2002). *Real world research: a resource for social scientists and practitioner-researchers* (2nd ed.). Blackwell Publishers.

Rodrigues Barbosa, E. (2013). La audiodescripción como herramienta para la enseñanza de ELE. In L. M. A. de Freitas (Ed.), *Anais do XIV Congresso Brasileiro de Professores de Espanhol: Língua e Ensino 1* (pp. 487-496). Rio de Janeiro: APEERJ. http://apeerj. blogspot.it/2013/07/anais-do-xiv-congresso-brasileiro-de.html

Rundle, C. (2000). Using subtitles to teach translation. In R. M. Bollettieri Bosinelli, C. Heiss, M. Soffritti & S. Bernardini (Eds), *La traduzione multimediale: quale traduzione per quale testo?* (pp. 167- 181). CLUEB.

Sánchez Requena, A. (2016). Audiovisual translation in teaching foreign languages: contributions of dubbing to develop fluency and pronunciation in spontaneous conversations. *Porta Linguarum*, *26*, 9-21. https://www.ugr.es/~portalin/articulos/PL_ numero26/ART1_Alicia%20Sanchez.pdf

Sánchez Requena, A. (2018). Intralingual dubbing as a tool for developing speaking skills. In L. Incalcaterra McLoughlin, J. Lertola & N. Talaván (Eds), *Special issue of Translation and Translanguaging in Multilingual Contexts. Audiovisual translation in applied linguistics: beyond case studies*, *4*(1), 102-128.

Shevchenko, N., & Blanco-Arnejo, M. (2005). *'Found in translation': how the Spanish 365 students taught Bart Simpson Spanish in a technology-enhanced language learning environment*. Bits, Bytes, & Nybbles.

Sokoli, S. (2015). ClipFlair: foreign language learning through interactive revoicing and captioning of clips. In Y. Gambier, A. Caimi & C. Mariotti (Eds), *Subtitles and language learning* (pp. 127-147). Peter Lang.

Sokoli, S. (2018). Exploring the possibilities of interactive audiovisual activities for language learning. In L. Incalcaterra McLoughlin, J. Lertola & N. Talaván (Eds), *Special issue of Translation and Translanguaging in Multilingual Contexts. Audiovisual translation in applied linguistics: beyond case studies*, *4*(1), 80-96.

Sokoli, S., Zabalbeascoa, P., & Fountana, M. (2011). Subtitling activities for foreign language learning: what learners and teachers think. In L. Incalcaterra McLoughlin, M. Biscio & M. Á. Ní Mhainnín (Eds), *Audiovisual translation subtitles and subtitling. Theory and practice* (pp. 219-242). Peter Lang.

Talaván, N. (2006a). Using subtitles to enhance foreign language education. *Porta linguarum, 6*, 41-52. https://www.ugr.es/~portalin/articulos/PL_numero6/talavan.pdf

Talaván, N. (2006b). The technique of subtitling for business English communication. *RLFE-Revista de Lenguas para Fines Específicos, 11/12*, 313-346.

Talaván, N. (2010). Subtitling as a task and subtitles as support: pedagogical applications. In J. Díaz Cintas, A. Matamala & J. Neves (Eds), *New insights into audiovisual translation and media accessibility* (pp. 285- 299). Rodopi.

Talaván, N. (2011). A quasi-experimental research project on subtitling and foreign language acquisition. In L. Incalcaterra McLoughlin, M. Biscio & M. Á. Ní Mhainnín (Eds), *Audiovisual translation subtitles and subtitling. Theory and practice* (pp. 197-217). Peter Lang.

Talaván, N. (2013). *La subtitulación en el aprendizaje de las lenguas extranjeras*. Octaedro.

Talaván, N., & Ávila-Cabrera, J. (2015). First insights into the combination of dubbing and subtitling as L2 didactic tools. In Y. Gambier, A. Caimi & C. Mariotti (Eds), *Subtitles and language learning* (pp. 149-172). Peter Lang.

Talaván, N., Bárcena, E., & Villarroel, A. (2014). Aprendizaje colaborativo asistido por ordenador para la transferencia de las competencias mediadora y lingüístico comunicativa en inglés especializado. In M. L. Pérez Cañado & J. Ráez Padilla (Eds), *Digital competence development in higher education: an international perspective* (pp. 87-106). Peter Lang.

Talaván, N., & Costal, T. (2017). iDub - The potential of intralingual dubbing in foreign language learning: how to assess the task. *Language Value, 9*(1), 62-88. http://www.languagevalue.uji.es/index.php/languagevalue/article/view/12/12

Talaván, N., Ibáñez, A., & Bárcena, E. (2016a). Exploring collaborative reverse subtitling for the enhancement of written production activities in English as a second language. *ReCALL, 29*(1), 39-58. https://doi.org/10.1017/S0958344016000197

Talaván, N., & Lertola, J. (2016). Active audiodescription to promote speaking skills in online environments. *Sintagma, 28*, 59-74. https://doi.org/10.21001/sintagma.2016.28.04

Talaván, N., Lertola, J., & Costal, T. (2016b). iCap: intralingual captioning for writing and vocabulary enhancement. *Alicante Journal of English Studies, 29*, 229-248. https://doi.org/10.14198/raei.2016.29.13

Talaván, N., & Rodríguez-Arancón, P. (2014a). The use of interlingual subtitling to improve listening comprehension skills in advanced EFL students. In B. Garzelli & M. Baldo (Eds), *Subtitling and intercultural communication. European languages and beyond* (pp. 273-288). InterLinguistica, ETS.

Talaván, N., & Rodríguez-Arancón, P. (2014b). The use of reverse subtitling as an online collaborative language learning tool. *Special issue of The Interpreter and Translator Trainer*, *8*(1), 84-101.

Talaván, N., & Rodríguez-Arancón, P. (forthcoming). Voice-over to improve oral production skills: the VICTOR project. In *Current Research on Audiovisual Translation*. Publicaciones Universitat de Valencia.

Talaván, N., Rodríguez-Arancón, P., & Martín-Monje, E. (2015). The enhancement of speaking skills practice and assessment in an online environment. In L. P. Cancelas y Ouviña & S. Sánchez Rodriguez (Eds), *Tendencias en educación y lingüística* (pp. 329-351). Editorial GEU.

Vanderplank, R. (2016). *Captioned media in foreign language learning and teaching: subtitles for the deaf and hard-of-hearing as tools for language learning*. Palgrave Macmillan. https://doi.org/10.1057/978-1-137-50045-8

Vermeulen, A. (2003). La traducción audiovisual en la enseñanza de idiomas. *Actas del Segundo Congreso Internacional de Español para Fines Específicos* (pp. 159-168). http://cvc.cervantes.es/ensenanza/biblioteca_ele/ciefe/indice2.htm

Wagener, D. (2006). Promoting independent learning skills using video on digital language laboratories. *Computer Assisted Language Learning, 19*(4-5), 279-286. https://doi.org/10.1080/09588220601043180

Wakefield, J. C. (2014). Dubbing as a method for language practice and learning. In C. DeCoursey (Ed.), *Language arts in Asia II: English and Chinese through literature, drama and popular culture* (pp. 160-166). Cambridge Scholars Publishing.

Walczak, A., & Szarkowska, A. (2012). Text-to-speech audio description of educational materials for visually impaired children. In S. Bruti & E. Di Giovanni (Eds), *Audiovisual translation across Europe: an ever-changing landscape* (pp. 209-234). Peter Lang.

Williams, H., & Thorne, D. (2000). The value of teletext subtitling as a medium for language learning. *System, 28*(2), 217-228. https://doi.org/10.1016/S0346-251X(00)00008-7

Yachi, M., & Karimata, E. (2008). Online video dubbing system for language education. In C. Bonk, M. Lee & T. Reynolds (Eds), *Proceedings of E-Learn 2008: world conference on e-learning in corporate, government, healthcare, and higher education* (pp. 4029-4034). Association for the Advancement of Computing in Education (AACE). https://www.learntechlib.org/p/30250/

Zabalbeascoa, P., Sokoli, S., & Torres, O. (2012). CLIPFLAIR foreign language learning through interactive revoicing and captioning of clips. Lifelong learning programme - Key activity 2. Languages, multilateral project. D2.1. Conceptual framework and pedagogical methodology. http://clipflair.net/wp-content/uploads/2014/06/D2.1ConceptualFramework.pdf

Zohrevandi, Z. (1994). Translation as a resource for teaching English as a foreign language. In R. de Beaugrande, A. Shunnaq & M. Heliel (Eds), *Language, discourse and translation in the West and Middle East* (pp. 181-187). John Benjamins. https://doi.org/10.1075/btl.7.25zoh

www.ingramcontent.com/pod-product-compliance
Lightning Source LLC
LaVergne TN
LVHW091726190726
843493LV00001B/464